50 WAYS TO HELP YOU WRITE

by Fran Shaw, Ph.D.

LONGMEADOW
PRESS

To my mother,
Elizabeth Weber,
with love always

Copyright Acknowledgments

Quotation from "The Harness," from The Long Valley by John Steinbeck.
Copyright 1938, renewed © 1966 by John Steinbeck. Used by permission of
Viking Penguin, a division of Penguin Books USA Inc.

Quotation from "Silent Snow, Secret Snow," by Conrad Aiken. Copyright 1932,
renewed © 1960 by Conrad Aiken. Used by permission of Brandt & Brandt
Literary Agents, Inc.

Quotations from "Confessions of a Female Chauvinist Sow," by Anne Roiphe,
from New York Magazine, October 1972. Copyright © 1972 by Anne Roiphe.
Used by permission of International Creative Management.

Cover design by Lisa Stokes

Interior design by Allan Mogel

Library of Congress Cataloging-in-Publication Data

Shaw, Fran Weber, 1947–
    50 ways to help you write / by Fran Shaw. — 1st ed.
       p.   cm.
    Includes index.
    ISBN: 0-681-00774-5
    1. Authorship.   I. Title.   II. Title: Fifty ways to help you
write.
    PN147.S466   1995
    808'.02—dc20   94-49324
                                                              CIP

Printed in the United States of America

First Edition

0 9 8 7 6 5 4 3 2 1

Contents

Part 3
FINDING YOUR WAY FROM NOTES TO FIRST DRAFT

Part 4
BECOMING YOUR OWN BEST EDITOR

Preface

When you put words on paper, is it like pulling teeth? You're not alone. Ask people what happens to them, and you'll hear: "I panic," "I can't get going," or "What comes out on the page just isn't as good as what's in my head."

But many of these same people are learning how to help themselves write, how to build confidence, save frustrating hours, and have a better time writing.

Would you like to:

—discover a way to write what you want anytime?
—get from first notes to final draft, painlessly?
—experience your creativity now?

These experiments are designed to give you a new ease and skill in writing. Try a few and you'll see you already have a wealth of material which can just pour out. You'll learn how to become your own best friend when you write. Instead of struggling, you can create a new condition from which words freely flow. You'll find the experiments especially useful if you're

—a student with an essay due

—a teacher trying to generate lively writing

—a businessperson who needs to communicate more effectively

—an aspiring writer who hopes to get going

—someone facing a writing task such as an important letter
to send.

People who have tried these experiments at schools, corporations, and writers' conferences tell me they have a fresh taste of words coming easily—and they're delighted with the results.

Whether you're a "non-writer" who must get a job done or an aspiring author who's feeling stuck, you'll find experiments here to suit your needs. Practice the ones that work best for you, and begin to build a new image of yourself: soon you'll know you, too, can write whatever you want.

Fran Shaw

WHAT DO YOU WANT TO WRITE?

ARTICLES AND ESSAYS

CREATIVE WRITING AND PERSONAL EXPLORATION

STORY WRITING

POETRY

HUMOR

ESPECIALLY FOR WRITING CLASSES

Note to Teachers: *For a change of pace, begin class with a writing experiment. Or suggest doing an experiment at home to generate material for assignments.*

Try Experiment

CREATIVE WRITING WORKSHOP
- tapping the unexpected, expanding
  awareness 1-4, 7-8, 12-16
- outdoor group poem 5
- stories, including experiments to try as
  a group to explore character, setting,
  theme, point of view, conflict, dialogue 9-11, 17-20
- poems of different kinds, including
  writing in class to music 6
- humor 22, 26
- peer review sheet for stories (see p. 49)

MAGAZINE WRITING WORKSHOP
- articles 21, 26, 27-29
- interviews 21, 25, 28
- oral history 28

BUSINESS WRITING
- startup sheet for document 30
- persuading with plain English 32

COMPOSITION

PART

1

NOTICING MORE AND HAVING PLENTY TO SAY

Introduction

Every time you sit down to write, you need to experience words coming easily. It feels good to sail across the page, something quickening inside as ideas pour out. And it's just this momentum that keeps you writing.

But how to begin? You've read, thought, made notes; you want to write. Yet you put it off all day. Finally, you sit down and eke out a few sentences . . . and then scrap them.

Sound familiar?

Look at it like this: you may be suffering from acute writing anxiety. The main symptom: believing the voice that jumps in to comment even *before* you begin ("I can't") and especially while you write ("This is no good"). It will stop you every time.

What a moment of possibility! Here's a sly way to avoid that, and get going. As an experiment, before you begin writing, turn your attention away from the task for a moment, and *focus on your body and senses now*. Doing this, you'll clear a space and make room for a fresh impulse.

You may notice that those thoughts which have you

stuck are mirrored in your physical self. Now as you read, for instance, are you holding your jaw tightly? Keep it like that a moment, then let it relax. Your new approach is as simple as that. While you give your body a few minutes of attention and relaxation, you're no longer fretting or criticizing. You're not stuck in that. Muscular tension slowly dissolves: you create a new condition in yourself.

"Try an experiment? Relax my face? Sounds interesting, but I haven't got time. I better just dig in and do it my old way."

You've heard that voice before. It's the one that makes you tense up. Once again you're about to, ugh, make spinach out of a writing task.

Why not save all those unproductive hours straining? Try an experiment; you'll discover things you didn't know a moment ago.

"Experimenting" means you don't know what will come. You open, in a specific way, to your experience and don't have to figure out what you'll write. In fact, by treating yourself like an undiscovered genius, you may discover your best ideas come when you're "playing" rather than forcing.

For now, don't edit or criticize *while you're writing*: that will happen later. At the moment, you want only to write abundantly without concerning yourself about impressing some future reader. Give yourself the chance to see how you can use the process of writing to feel more alive and express that intensity.

Whatever you want to write, take ten pleasant minutes now to try a first experiment.

Experiment 1
Write free-flow for the pleasure of now

"Now I'm Sitting Here and"	1. Sit comfortably, perhaps outdoors. Write across the top of your pad: "NOW I'M SITTING HERE AND." Put down your pad and pen. Read steps 2, 3, and 4, and try them.
Relax, Head to Toe	2. Close your eyes, and allow the muscles of your face to relax. Move down your body, naming to yourself each part and suggesting it relax. (Don't worry about how much you can relax—that's not important.)
Listen	3. REALLY LISTEN to sounds from all directions, as if nothing else matters but hearing everything.
Write Nonstop	4. Very slowly open your eyes. Pick up your pen and start "TALKING" nonstop on the page. When you don't know what to say next, DESCRIBE sounds, smells, tastes, tactile sensations, and sights. Keep your pen moving for two pages, and then stop.
	5. Read through, and underline key words or phrases or whatever strikes you.

Did you notice
   —how it is possible for you to cover a page with words?
   —how to build momentum?
   —where in your writing you sound really sure?
   —if more is available to you when you're not harnessed to a task but free to explore in any direction?

4

Here's a sample by someone who's done a lot of free-flow writing. The writer tried Experiment 1 by a waterfall:

Watching from a log above the falls. Below, white water coursing in all directions, pushing through rocks for an outlet. I'm noticing the rise and fall of my chest, a fly darting about, the heat of the sun on my arms. . . .

She cast it into the third person to see if it suggests a story:

A rush of waters. Jenny watched from a log above the falls. Below, white water coursed in all directions, pushing through rocks for an outlet.

Try Experiment 1 using the phrase "THIS MOMENT" as your springboard. Write ten minutes a day for a week, at different hours or in favorite places. Begin an Album of You. Or write this way while music plays. You'll notice each time you do that conditions within you seem different. It's a new current you're feeling and the current is strong!

The more you try, the more you see how to build momentum. You'll write some surprisingly well-turned phrases, and gain confidence.

BUT WHAT ABOUT THOSE 500 WORDS DUE FRIDAY?

If you have an essay, report, proposal, or letter to write, get going by FINDING THE QUESTION you are able to answer. Turn to Experiment 48, p. 161, to discover how to write 500 words about anything.

Where else should you look for material? As you try experiments and begin writing an essay or story, ideas for other things to write may come to you. Don't let them slip by. What someone says may spark a memory, or you'll

5

overhear a bit of conversation—a new subject will probably occur to you. Before going back to what you're working on, jot down a few lines on anything handy; later, put it in an "Ideas" folder. Or you may read something that interests you in a newspaper or magazine: a funny incident, a statistic, a scientific discovery, an unusual item about a person or event or pet subject. Tear out the article and put it in a "Clippings" folder. Don't count on remembering: always record your idea. When you feel like writing, you can look through these folders for stimulation.

Even more stimulating is a vivid, heightened experience now which will give you plenty to say, and get you in motion. Choose one of the next five experiments, and try it step by step.

Experiment 2
Walk "blind" to discover more

1. Ask someone to talk you on a Blind Walk.[1] Cover your eyes with a scarf. Your guide takes you by the hand.
2. WALK BLINDFOLDED in silence. Let your guide hand you things to touch.
3. After ten minutes, take off your blindfold but keep your eyes closed. SIT down and SENSE the palms of your hands . . .
4. Very slowly OPEN your eyes just a crack at first, then halfway. Eyes open, look at your hands. Freely WRITE your experience from beginning to end.

Did you notice
—what you felt when you took your first steps, and how this feeling changed?

---

[1] A technique for expanding awareness, suggested in Lewis and Streitfeld's *Growth Games* (New York: Bantam Books, 1970).

—which of your senses seemed to be working more?

—your first thought or visual impression when you opened your eyes?

—anything new about something familiar, as if experiencing it for the first time?

Experiment 3
Continuously sense each step

1. STAND for a moment SENSING the contact of your feet and the ground. Sense your toes, ball of your foot, arch, heel. (You can try this barefoot if you like, or with one shoe off.)
2. WALK for five minutes, trying to be aware, through sensation, of each foot touching the ground. When something distracts you, focus again.
3. STAND for a moment, still aware of your feet on the ground. RETURN, knowing each footstep.
4. Sit down, and WRITE across the top of a page: "I was walking." Midway down the page write: "And then it happened."
5. WRITE NONSTOP completing the first sentence. When you get halfway down the page, let your imagination take over. Keep writing! Stop after two pages.

Did you notice

—how many times you really had a sense of your feet and the ground? what took you away?

—anything unusual about the surface you walked on?

—how walking with a focus helps you experience more?

Experiment 4
Look for one color

1. Take a Yellow Walk or a White Walk. That is, as you walk, look for things of one color.
2. The instant you notice something yellow, it's as if a camera clicks, and you're in the picture. Write down what you see and also something about yourself now (how you're standing, your facial expression, what you're thinking or feeling).
3. Walk for ten minutes making notes.
4. Sit down, read what you have, and WRITE NON-STOP. Describe your walk from beginning to end, or perhaps write a poetic catalogue of all these things of one color.

Did you notice
   —*if you saw more when trying to look for one color?*
   —*whether any objects reminded you of another time or place?*
   —*anything in nature that seemed to "say" something about your life?*

SHAPING WHAT COMES

Your free-flow writings may become part of a story or essay, so keep them (as is) in your "writings" notebook. You'll find you'll accumulate a wealth of personal material, which is your own natural resource. One woman, for example, "mined" her notebook and arranged seven short pieces as one "crisis" week in her character's life. A businessman was able to use a whimsical bit as the opening anecdote for a speech. So keep writing for the fun of it—without criticizing what comes—and you'll have something to work with when you need material.

If you'd like to take one of your writings and shape it into a paragraph or short essay, try this:

1. Choose a piece you really like, and read it over.
2. What did you realize from this experience? Sum up your MAIN IMPRESSION in a sentence and say it out loud as if telling a friend.
3. Begin a new paragraph each time you bring in another idea, shift gears, or describe something happening suddenly.
4. Cross out in pencil any details or sentences which don't have anything to do with the main impression you want to convey.
5. End with a sentence you sound sure of. Make your point about what you've discovered. Title this piece, and type it up.

If you'd like to begin a story, try this:

1. Name your main character.
2. Cast your free-flow writing into the third person (use *he* or *she*), and see if it suggests a story. Now it's your main character that's sitting, or walking, or thinking about things, or noticing the surroundings.
3. Try to convey a particular mood by the way your character sees what's around, by what she's thinking. Cross out sentences that don't fit. Add others which might suggest what her problem or situation is at this moment.
4. Write just the first page of your story. Rather than plan what you'll say, let it unfold: just keep writing.

A word about point of view. Your point of view reveals your impression or appraisal of an experience. It's like a particular pair of glasses that tints what you see a certain color. The reader sees the world through your eyes. Also, a point of view can orient your reader in time and space: you view a scene from a specific point on a hillside on a summer morning, for instance, and describe the panorama. Or, your point of view can be your feeling about an experience. For example, walking blindfolded terrified you at first, and each step meant danger. Or, in a story, the point of view has to do with which character you let witness and tell what happens. Does the young widow tell her own story, in diary form, or is the story told from the point of view of her teenage son?

That is, do you write in the first person (*I*), the second person (*you*), or the third (*he, she, one, it*)? It's important not to jump around too much. If you choose *I*, don't shift to *you*. Don't write: *I* never realized how little I notice of the world around me. *You* don't hear or see half of what's happening." If you write, "*He* watched the sunlight play on the leaves," don't add, "*You* could see each vein."

A reminder: when shaping these first writings, be faithful to your experience and to the voice in which you first expressed it. Your own voice has power. A quality of emotion comes through, a rhythm of words that holds the writing together.

Here's how one professional writer shaped material from a walk. In his story, a boy comes home from school. What main impression comes through—in a word, how does the world look to the boy?

Twigs of bushes leaned over the walls; the little hard green winterbuds of lilac, on gray stems, sheathed and fat; other branches very thin and fine and black and desiccated. Dirty sparrows huddled in the bushes, as dull in color as dead fruit left in leafless trees. A single starling creaked on a weather vane. In the gutter, beside a drain, was a scrap of torn and dirty newspaper, caught in a little delta of filth. . . .

(from Conrad Aiken's
"Silent Snow, Secret Snow")

FREEING MATERIAL FOR ALL KINDS OF WRITING

Chapter 1

Describing People, Places, and Things

When you don't know what to write, or can't find the words, consider whether your senses are working at full pressure.

A rich sensory experience yields a wealth of simultaneous impressions which call for words to convey that intensity. A writing experiment can help you discover the route to greater experience so you'll find your way whenever your material seems insufficient.

It's best to start simply. Take your cue, as I do, from the haiku poets who express in only seventeen syllables a powerful moment of experience. It's something like taking a snapshot of what is right now, without being general or abstract, such as Gyodai's haiku:

Snow is melting . . .
  Far in the misted mountains
    a caw-cawing crow.[1]

---

[1] Quoted in *Cherry Blossoms* (Mt. Vernon, New York, 1960), p. 7.

It's almost as if it's the poet's role to be the eyes and ears by which the universe perceives itself.

By writing short imagist or haiku poems, you stretch your descriptive abilities and see how to focus on the startling particular.

To feel your senses opening more, first take five minutes for yourself and allow a wave of relaxation to flow through you. Practice this so you can do it any time:

RELAXATION EXERCISE

Sit comfortably, and close your eyes.

Allow the muscles of your face to RELAX. Move slowly down your body, silently relaxing each part from HEAD to TOE.

LISTEN a while to sound coming in from all directions, as if nothing else matters but doing that.

Slowly open your eyes, and do a writing experiment.

Experiment 5
Write "three-liners" to notice what's here

You can try this experiment by yourself or with others.

1. Go to a favorite place outdoors. Open with your relaxation exercise (above).
2. Without turning your head, notice what's in your peripheral vision along with what's in front of you.
3. Write phrases, one on each line, in groups of three lines, that convey vivid details of this place now.

Try this with others to create a "group" poem:

4. Choose your best three short poems and number them one, two, three.

5. Move into a circle. Have each person read aloud her number one, going around the circle. Go around again, reading number 2, and then around once more, reading number 3.

Did you notice
   —if you captured the flavor of the season?
   —which poems seem like snapshots?
   —how many of your senses came into your writing?
   —a sequence in what you wrote? would you rearrange?

Here's part of a group sequence written one summer morning at the beach.

from BEACHWRITING

Hot sand,
   a radio blaring;
      a wave rolls in and breaks.

      Shadows of a leg, an arm;
         warm breeze and salt smell;
            effortless birds.

As you discovered from Experiment 5, even if you don't think of yourself as a poet, once you open to the experience of your senses, words flow onto the page. There is much in you waiting to be said!

To compose a poem, I compose myself. Can I begin to be attentive to impressions of body, senses, and surroundings? Engaging in writing poetry this way can expand awareness. The secret, of course, is that you continually refresh this awareness, making it always more important than the words.

14

Experiment 6
Compose a poem sixteen ways

Writing from Expanded Awareness:

1. Sit quietly OUTDOORS in a favorite place where you can close your eyes. LISTEN to sounds all around. Become aware of your breathing, and count to yourself as you follow with your attention TEN BREATHS. . . . Slowly open your eyes. Describe in a poem what you perceive now, "what is."

2. MEDITATE for twenty minutes. Still aware of your breathing, slowly open your eyes. Put a few words on the page which come from an inner quiet. If words start the mind associating and you lose this connection, pause, and become aware again in the same way as when you were meditating. Then write a few more words. Pause . . . Breathe . . . Feel your presence here. Write a few more words. Pause . . . Breathe . . . Write . . . Pause . . .

3. Go outside or sit by the window. Notice your breathing. Without turning your head, become aware of your peripheral VISION, what's at your far left and far right. And listen. What strikes you most about this place?
   a. Write an IMAGIST poem, letting the images alone express a particular feeling about life or about someone in this moment.
   b. Try writing in the compressed form of the HAIKU: 17 syllables divided into 3 lines of 5, 7, and 5 syllables.

4. Collect some OBJECTS and place them on the floor. If you're in a writing class, have everyone bring in something (e.g., a shell, a bowl, a necklace).
   a. Sit quietly for a moment, and try to become aware of the whole of yourself from the top of your head to your seat

on the chair to the soles of your feet . . . Listen . . . Breathe . . .

b. (OPTIONAL) Put on some quiet instrumental music in the background.
c. Look at the objects. Touch them. Does any one object attract you or suggest something you can write about? Begin your poem with a description of this object.

Writing by Stimulating the Mind:

5. Write a poem on an "UNPOETIC" subject (e.g., bathrooms, calculus).
6. Write a poem using TEN RANDOM WORDS. If you're in a writing class, have everyone instantly offer a word. Or pick ten words at random from a magazine or dictionary. Compose a poem using all ten words.
7. Find a NEWSPAPER STORY about a dramatic event involving one or two people. Narrate it as poem as if you were a reporter on the scene, telling who, what, when, where, how. What does the poem make you feel about human nature or the human condition?

Writing from Dreams, Emotions, and Inner Journeys:

8. Keep a dream journal next to your bed, and write in it first thing in the morning for a week. Describe in poetic form a DREAM.
9. Write a LOVE POEM to someone you love.
10. Try any of the GUIDED Experiments 12–15, pp. 30–37. Use highlights in your free-flow writing in a poem which describes a "peak" moment.

Writing by Reading Poetry:

11. Write an IMITATION of another poet's work using your own subject.
    a. Make a study of that poet. Read several poems; write down repeated words and images. Notice what poetic devices this

16

poet uses. Words with the vowel *i*? Long or short lines? Images of light?

b. Use a favorite poem as a model. You choose the subject, but imitate the form (line length, rhyme scheme, etc.).

c. Write a stanza using the "repeat and vary" pattern in the Whitman poem on p. 177. That is, for several lines, repeat the first words of the line but change the last words. How does this create a sense of something building?

12. Write a PARODY of a poem or song. Exaggerate the poet's style for humorous effect. If the poet uses overly long lines, make yours really long. If what the poet or song writer expresses is overly sentimental or banal, overdo it even more.

Having Fun with Poetic Forms:

13. Write your SHORT STORY as a rhymed poem. Or, for humor, summarize a famous short story or novel in a poem.

14. Write several funny LIMERICKS (rhyme scheme AABBA).

Sample Form for Your Limerick

There was an old fellow from yuh-dum (A)
Who wandered away from his tuh-dum (A)
He met a dee-day (B)
And then went dee-hay (B)
And now he can never duh-yuh-dum (A)

15. Write a SONNET (fourteen lines of rhymed iambic pentameter ending in a couplet). Look at some sonnets in an anthology. Be sure to follow the conventions of that form (the correct number of stresses per line, the pattern of the rhymes, etc.).

SUGGESTION: Write about a relationship, a memory, a feeling, a place. Save your "clincher" (what it all means) for the ending couplet.

Writing to Music, with Springboards:

16. Write to instrumental MUSIC of different kinds, especially music with strong emotional impact. Change the tape or CD about every ten minutes.

a. Eyes closed, relax your body as you just listen to music that touches the emotions. What images and phrases occur to you?
b. Begin to write a poem to the music.
c. If you like, use any of the FIRST WORDS or OPENING LINES below as a takeoff point. Allow yourself to look at the list from time to time, or when you change the music.

OPENING LINES:

Let us go now

I give in. I must not

In the night-reaches

These lovely

Halfway to death

Leaving behind

He had been falling

Like a

In sleep she knew

With these words escaping

Suppose I chose

There's a private matter

A sad light gleams

Much have I traveled

How was it that she

From that moment

Time has cast

A distant sound

Did you notice
—specific suggestions help you tap into what's waiting to be said?
—music can bring images to get you going?
—a lovely or unusual turn of phrase can just appear, once you're in motion?
—you enjoy writing poetry?
—you have a new direction to explore in your poetry?

Experiment 7
Where am I?

1. Go to a place which is special to you. Open with your relaxation exercise (p. 13).
2. WALK through the area, and TOUCH or pick up five things. Each time, be aware of the contact of your hand with that surface or object.
3. Sit down and MAKE A LIST of 25 sensory specifics of the place you're in, trying for five sights, sounds, tastes, smells, textures.
4. If you like, read this list aloud to people, and ask them to guess the location. Ask which words give it away.

Did you notice
   —anything new about your favorite place?
   —whether you have more material from one or two senses than from others?
   —if you found just the right words to describe this setting and no other?

Experiment 8
Guess who's being described

This experiment is designed to sharpen your observation of details so that you can convey on paper the kind of image a photograph would capture. Aside from testing your ability to portray a person, you can use this experiment to create a character for a story.

1. CLIP A PICTURE of someone famous. Study the person's facial expression, build, hair, and clothing.
2. CLOSE your eyes for a moment, and relax a little more with each outbreath. OPEN your eyes. Look at the picture. What strikes you first?
3. Write that as your first sentence. Continue describing this person from head to toe. Look at the picture often.
4. Try this with others: DESCRIBE someone in the room without naming the person. Write down ten words or phrases; list the most striking feature last.
5. READ your characterization aloud. How soon can others guess who's being described? Which words give it away?

Did you notice
   —if you've written a "photographic" description?
   —what sort of details are more vivid and telling than others?
   —if facial expression, pose, or clothing suggest to you a story about this person? can you write the first paragraph now?

WHAT HAVE YOU BEEN WANTING TO EXPLORE IN YOUR WRITING?

During this "creative stage," when you're trying to "grow a story" from your experience, don't worry about editing or polishing. For the next few experiments, your only goal is WRITE ABUNDANTLY and without criticizing.

Experiment 9
Create a character

1. Fill in: *I want to write about a* _____
   who _____ *(wants what? does what?)*
   but who _____ *(finds what? is blocked by what? discovers what?).*

Write four different sentences. Pick the story idea with the character you most want to work with now.

2. Fill in: What does this person most DESIRE and what are the OBSTACLES in the way?

    OUTER: Wants what in the world? _____
                Blocked by what outside? _____

    INNER: Really needs what emotionally? _____
                Blocked by what inside? _____

3. Do a CHARACTERISTICS CHART. List these categories down the left side of the page, quickly pick a name for your character, and fill in phrases for the rest:

Name	Schools
Nickname	Role model
Age	Favorite food
Height	Favorite expression
Weight or build	Travels
Looks like	Dreams
Hair color and style	Loves
Typical clothes	Background
Occupation	Childhood
Hometown	Wants most of all
Current home	Unfinished emotional business
Family	from the past
Jobs	

TIP: If you're concerned that your character is too much like yourself or someone you know, drastically CHANGE one important physical detail or add one physical flaw.

4. Describe your character doing something TYPICAL. Include in your paragraph "telling details" of appearance, clothing, posture, gesture, tone of voice, and facial expression. Write with vivid sensory specifics of color, shape, texture, sound, and smell.

TIP: You may or may not use the paragraph as a whole in your story. Sometimes lengthy description can slow down the action. If that's the case, just choose single sentences to use as dialogue tags so we see the character while staying with the action.

5. Describe the OBJECTS on the night table next to your character's bed.
6. Use as a MODEL a famous writer's description of a character. Insert your own content into the form of the sentences to make it your own.

Did you notice
  —*the details poured out once you named your character and began the list?*
  —*that you did know exactly what was on this character's night table?*
  —*that wanting things in the outside world is only part of what the character really wants and needs?*

Experiment 10
Sketch someone without explaining

1. CHOOSE or MAKE UP one striking personality trait for your character, and write it out. Such as:
   Joel made jokes to cover up his shyness.
   Adele thought she wanted money more than anything.
2. CLOSE your eyes, for a moment, and picture your character in motion, walking out of the house, or into a party or board meeting. What does she notice first? What does she do? Can you see the expression on her face? What's she like with others?
3. OPEN your eyes. WRITE the first page of the story. BEGIN by describing your character going somewhere or arriving. DRAMATIZE her main trait so you see and hear her. Show how she's feeling through her

—walk (determined stride, or hesitating?)
—posture (slouching, or standing tall?)
—gesture (cigarette poised, or hands waving as she talks?)
—tone of voice (whining, or authoritarian?)
—clothing (starched, or top button open?)
—facial expression (knitted brows, or beaming?)

SHOW, rather than explain.

Did you notice
—*whether you know your character well? Could you see and hear her once you set her in motion?*

Experiment 11
Explore your setting

Version 1: Explore where you are right now

1. Make up a CHART with these headings at the top of each column:

        What does this place
look like? Sound like? Smell like? Taste like? Feel like to touch?

2. OPEN to this place: sense the contact of your seat on the chair, lower your eyes to rest on a point in front of you, and LISTEN to all the sounds around you.
3. Fill in the chart with sensory phrases that DESCRIBE the room you're in now. What does this room look like? Sound like?

Version 2: Explore a location in your story

1. Make a second CHART with the same headings as in the first step above.
2. Write down a PLACE where a scene from your story occurs (*Marisa's kitchen; a field in Spain*).

3. Do the RELAXING EXERCISE from head to toe: CLOSE your EYES. Starting at the top of your head, slowly move your attention down through your body, letting go of the tension in your face, shoulders, chest, abdomen, arms, and legs.
4. "GO" to that place in your story and notice everything. What strikes you first? What colors? What sounds? Move your gaze from right to left so you "see" it all.
5. Open your eyes and DRAW a sketch of that place: what's there?
6. Fill in your CHART with sensory specifics describing the place in your story.
7. Write a PARAGRAPH describing the setting. Be sure your main CHARACTER or NARRATOR is there.

Describe the place in any of these ways: most striking detail first; from far to near; as if walking into it; from right to left; emphasizing colors, smells, or sounds; with series of objects.

Version 3: Vary your sentences to get the "atmosphere" you want

1. Pick a MOOD for your character (irritable, angry, in love, nervous). Write about the setting so we know (without being told) what that mood is.

For instance, your character is worried so everything looks gray and gloomy. Or, your character's mood conflicts with the setting: it's bright and sunny, but she's irritable and thinks, "Why does it have to be so sunny!"

TIP: To show mood, show body language. Is he slumped over? Frowning? Tapping his fingers on the table?

2. Try a series of sentence FRAGMENTS, phrases without verbs (*Clumps of dirty snow on the porch. Glaring sunlight.*).

TIP: If your character is nervous, or the action rapid-fire, use sentence fragments to give a choppy, unsettled "feel" to the paragraph.

24

3. Try one or two very long "flowing" sentences. Which sentences can you COMBINE? What effect does that give you?
4. Do a CATALOGUE of OBJECTS (*a cracked mirror, papers strewn on the desk, an empty glass . . .*).
5. Include a LIST of very detailed COLORS.

BONUS EXPERIMENT: *Looking at Landscape Paintings to Suggest a Story*

1. Look through a big BOOK of landscape paintings (surrealist, impressionist, your choice). Choose any "place" you see that attracts you, and leave that page open in front of you.
2. Close your eyes. Let go of the tension in your face and jaw. Notice the light coming in behind closed lids. Slowly open your eyes, and look at the page.
3. Describe that place or just write NONSTOP what happens there. Write a one-page short story.

Did you notice
   —*expanding your awareness of a place lets more into your writing?*
   —*details come to the forefront which you hadn't noticed before?*
   —*you can convey precisely the atmosphere you want through the right detail and the right rhythm of words?*

SHAPING WHAT COMES
DESCRIBING A PLACE

You have written down many sensory details of a particular location, perhaps in the form of a list or a free-flow passage. What's most striking about this place, if you had to single out one thing? What first caught your eye? What main impression would you like to convey?

For instance, you're describing a room, and you want it to seem elegant. You'd include details such as polished teak floors, gold doorknobs, filigreed tables, but omit yellowing drapes. If you intend to give the impression of "elegant-but-fading," you could use all those details.

Obvious ways of picturing a place are from a physical point of view, that is, from left to right, top to bottom, focal point to periphery, near to far (or the reverse of any of these). Zoom in like a camera. First, the front of the house, the fence, the walk, the porch, the front door, the entrance hall, the stairs.

There's another way to tie together details. Your strong feeling about a setting would lend unity to a more "impressionistic" portrayal. Perhaps you wrote what struck you first, what thoughts stirred, what something reminded you of. If you're imagining a messy room, for instance, perhaps you don't want to write an orderly (right to left) description. Or, if you're trying to build suspense, you might send your imagination down a dark hallway and have a bat suddenly fly out. The point is: what works? What effect do you want to create, and does this arrangement of sentences bring out that feeling?

To sum up, when you shape your description:

1. Discover the main impression you want to create.
2. Decide on the main feeling you have to convey.
3. Arrange sensory specifics to make the description build.
4. Cross out any details that don't contribute to your main impression.
5. Read aloud. Does this place come alive? Title your piece, and type it up.

NOW, WHAT COULD HAPPEN HERE?

Try another version of your description. Imagine this place while something's going on. Two lovers enter. Or a man running. Write nonstop and see what happens.

If you're writing a story, EXPRESS THE MOOD OF A CHARACTER by bringing out details of the environment. For instance, you might use any of the following details describe a crowded street corner: sunlit, bright, smiling faces, smell of chestnuts roasting. That same corner, when you're tired or if you just got yelled at, might suggest these words: glaring, loud, jostled, frowns, over-dressed, too much make-up, zombies, chilly wind, treeless. How subjectively we see the world at any moment! So if your main character is "in a state," select from all the details of a place those which reflect his "inner landscape" as well.

Try this: CONVEY THE MOOD of a character by showing how he sees this place you've described. Add or alter details to suggest how he feels.

For example:
— a boy walking home sees only what's dirty.
— a man waits nervously.
— she's exhausted after a fight with him.
— she's got a crush on the new teacher.

Make up your own character and situation, then try describing a locale from his point of view. Does the world look beautiful or hostile? What thoughts interject themselves? Write nonstop the first page of a story. What could happen next? Keep going until something is resolved.

DESCRIBING A PERSON

How does he or she look, sound, smell, eat, dress, walk? What strikes you first? Strength? Sexiness? What gives that impression?

Also, if you're creating a character for a story, what qualities about her fascinate? Think of favorite characters in books or films: what traits appeal? Good-natured humor? Persistence in the face of obstacles?

Your portrayal could focus on one main feature and include many sensory details. Using the material you've generated:

1. Make a note of what one strong characteristic impresses you.
2. Select details of appearance which stand out.
3. Show this person doing something typical or revealing: walking, talking to a friend, busy working at something.
4. Cross out items which don't add to the impression you're creating.
5. Does this person come alive? Can you see him? Type up.

You can weave in background information even as you give vivid sensory details. Here's an example from W. Somerset Maugham's novel *The Razor's Edge* (1949). English interior decorator Gregory Brabazon visits a rich American family, the Bradleys. Can you see him in their garish drawing room?

He was a short, very fat man, as bald as an egg except for a ring of black curly hair round his ears and at the back of his neck, with a red naked face that looked as though it were on the point of breaking out into a violent sweat, quick gray eyes, sensual lips and a heavy jowl. He was very jovial, very hearty and laughed a great deal, but you didn't have to be a great judge of character to know that his noisy friendliness was merely cover for a very astute man of business. He had been for some years the most successful decorator in London. He had a great booming voice and little fat hands that were wonderfully expressive. With telling gestures, with a spate of excited words he could thrill the imagination of a doubting client . . .

. . . I caught the professional look he gave the room as he came in and the involuntary lifting of his bushy eyebrows. It was indeed an amazing room. The paper on the walls, the cretonne of the curtains and on the upholstered furniture were of the same pattern; on the walls were oil paintings in massive gold frames that the Bradleys had evidently bought when they were in Rome. Virgins of the school of Raphael, Virgins of the school of Guido Reni, landscapes of the school of Zuccarelli, ruins of the school of Pannini . . . The lampshades were of white silk on which some ill-advised artist had painted shepherds and shepherdesses in Watteau costumes. It was hideous and yet, I don't know why, agreeable . . .

You'll notice that this description says something about Brabazon, the Bradleys, and the narrator as well.

Chapter 2

Showing What Happened

These next experiments open wide the floodgates! People like them because they generate interesting writing painlessly. Often one taps a flow, strikes a rich vein. What comes may surprise you.

You can direct yourself once you've tried these experiments, but for the first time it's useful just to let yourself go into the experience: have someone read the script while you relax with eyes closed. Try these at home with a friend helping you (but not when you're tired, or you'll fall asleep).

These next experiments are especially for people who want to free some material for stories.

Experiment 12
Invite intense moments

Do this with a friend directing you (and others if you like). Find a carpeted quiet room. If you need to mask sounds, play music softly in the background (the second movement of Beethoven's Sixth works well). Keep a notebook and pen ready by your side.

Your "guide" will elaborate on these steps:

1. LIE DOWN on your back.
2. CLOSE YOUR EYES and RELAX your face and body, moving down slowly from head to toe.
3. "GO" to a place where you've had an INTENSE MOMENT, and watch what happens there.
4. RETURN, open your eyes slowly, sit up, and WRITE NONSTOP what happened from beginning to end.

INSTRUCTIONS AND SCRIPT FOR YOUR GUIDE

Speak in a soothing quiet voice. Relax your body along with the experimenter(s) so you don't hurry. If there's background music, be sure it plays very quietly. Read aloud the parts in quotation marks (" "). Dots (. . .) mean to *pause*. Instructions for you are given in brackets [ ]. Tell your experimenter(s) to put pads and pens close by.

1. *"LIE DOWN on your back. Let the whole weight of your body sink into the floor. . . . Now you're beginning to relax. Starting with the top of your head, let a wave of relaxation sweep down your body. Your forehead relaxes. . . .*
2. *"RELAX your face . . . around the eyes. . . . Your jaw relaxes . . . your neck. . . .*
   [Continue moving slowly down, naming out loud each part of the body, and suggesting it relax.]
3. *"NOW, like an actor summoning a past experience, 'GO' to a place where you've had an intense moment. . . . You felt something powerful. . . . Where are you? . . . What colors? . . . What do you hear? . . . WATCH yourself MOVE through the scene to the end.*
   [Wait at least 5 minutes before continuing.]
4. *"When you're ready, you can come back to this room. . . . Very slowly, allow your eyes to open. . . . Sit up. . . . Pick up your pad and pen, and write as fast as you can to get it all down. Tell what happened from beginning to end. Go!"*

Did you notice
   —*which of your senses were stirred during this experience?*
   have you conveyed all those vivid sensory details?
   —*where in your writing there's a sense of something building?*
   —*if you learned something about life? could you use this*
   material in an autobiographical essay?
   —*if you have a setting for a story here or a possible main*
   character in some emotional state?

The next experiment, "Travel through time," brings out
unusual writing and sometimes startling experiences. Some
people find themselves "in a different body" moving through
a place they've never been. And yet they can recapture it all in
such detail!

For example, one woman saw herself as a young boy
holding his mother's hand as they walked toward an island
village. She used this material as a dream sequence in a story
she was writing about a woman who felt her parents always
wanted a son not a daughter.

Whatever your experience, your description will be
vivid, with a quality of immediacy that's engaging. You'll be
in control of your "travels" even as you watch them unfold.

Experiment 13
Travel through time[1]

Your guide will tell you these steps:

1. LIE DOWN on your back, CLOSE your EYES, and relax from
   head to toe.

---

[1]This experiment was inspired by a procedure described in William Glaskin's fascinating book *Windows of the Mind* (New York: Delacorte Press).

2. VISUALIZE stretching out through the soles of your feet and the top of your head as if your body is getting longer; "expand all over" like a balloon.
3. PICTURE your house from the roof looking down, and then go higher so you can see the neighborhood. "TRAVEL."
4. "Land" on solid ground, feet first, and NOTICE what's around and how you're dressed.
5. When ready, sense your back on the floor, open your eyes, and WRITE free-flow every detail of what happened.

SCRIPT FOR YOUR GUIDE

—If you want to mask outside noises, play softly a tape of Beethoven's *Pastoral*, 2nd movement, and Aaron Copland's "Corral Nocturne" (from *Rodeo*), or any quiet background music.
—Dots . . . mean to pause. Brackets [] enclose instructions for the guide.
—Tell experimenter(s) to sit on the floor with pad and pen close by.

1. *"LIE DOWN on your back . . . close your eyes. Allow all of your weight to sink into the floor. . . . Starting at the top of your head, a wave of relaxation flows down your body. Relax your forehead . . . around the eyes . . . your cheeks . . . your ears . . . your jaw relaxes. . . .* [Continue moving down, suggesting each part relax.]
2. *"Now VISUALIZE your feet as you lie here. Imagine them growing out six inches through the bottoms, as if your body has become longer by six inches. . . . Can you stretch six inches through your feet? . . . Now focus on the top of your head. . . . Stretch out six inches through there, as if you are six inches longer. . . . Can you stretch out through the top of your head? . . . Now expand all over, like a balloon, front and back, top and bottom and sides. . . . You're whole body is very light, very porous. . . . Now, you're ready to travel. . . .*
3. *"PICTURE the roof of this building, looking down at it. Go up higher, so you can see the whole neighborhood. Whatever time of day it is, put the scene in full daylight. . . . Go higher. . . . Now the landscape is*

far below, and you begin to TRAVEL across the surface of the planet, watching what passes below. . . . [Pause a minute.]

4. "Look for solid ground to come down on . . . feet first on a dry spot. . . . Land . . . Glance at your feet: Are you barefoot? What are you wearing on them? . . . Look around. Where are you? . . . Any people? . . . Begin walking. Is there a path? . . . Keep walking. What do you see? . . . Hear? . . . Follow where the path leads, noticing everything you can. . . . [Allow three minutes.]

5. "When you're ready to return, sense your back against the floor. . . . Listen for the sounds of this room. . . . Sense the length of your body on the floor. . . . Slowly open your eyes, and sit up. . . . Take your pad and pen, and WRITE NONSTOP getting down every detail from beginning to end."

Did you notice
  —a quality of immediacy and vividness in your account?
  —if you could begin a story with this material? or do you have a flashback or dream sequence for a story?
  —if at some point you felt you were about to discover something?
  —how much material you have access to when you explore in a new way? do you feel there's more you could tap?

Experiment 14
Take a bird's-eye view[2]

Your guide will tell you these steps:

1. LIE DOWN, close your eyes, let tensions drain down and out.
2. IMAGINE your body getting denser, heavier, like a rock . . . and then more porous, lighter, like a feather.

[2]Based on suggestions in Masters and Houston's *Mind Games* (Delta, 1972).

3. CHANGE shape, grow wings, like a bird.
4. "FLY" to music.
5. Return, open your eyes, and WRITE NONSTOP describing your flight.

SCRIPT FOR YOUR GUIDE

For this experiment light flowing music is essential. Choose a piece which evokes the outdoors, such as "Lever du Jour" from Ravel's *Daphnis and Chloe*. Turn it on after step 4.

Instruct experimenter(s) to put pads and pens next to them on the floor and:

1. *"LIE DOWN on your back, and close your eyes. Let your face relax . . . and allow a wave of relaxation to flow down your body, relaxing face, jaw, neck.* [Continue down the body, slowly, naming each part and suggesting relaxation.] *Let the floor support the whole weight of your body.*
2. *"Your body is getting lighter, more porous, like a feather floating just above the floor. . . . Now you feel the air on your skin, it's as if the air can move right through you. . . .*
3. *"You see how you can be any size and shape, even another life form. Now change shape, getting smaller . . . your arms become wings . . . and you're taking the form of a bird. . . . Sense the air against your body. It's as if it lifts you, you're getting lighter. . . . A breeze blows in through the open window, and now you can fly right out of this room. . . .*
4. *"You're above this building now . . . you're rising higher . . . notice the . . . what do you see? . . . where are you flying to? . . . Let the music take you. . . .* [Turn on MUSIC. Allow five minutes. Decrease volume just before speaking again.]
5. *"When you're ready, you can return to your normal size and shape. . . . Sense your back on the floor here in this room. . . . Allow your eyes to open slowly, sit up. . . . Take pen and pad, and SKETCH IN WORDS your flight from beginning to end in phrases or images; write one on each line, like a poem."* [Put music on again, from the beginning, quietly as background.]

Did you notice

— *if you have the last line for a story, giving the impression that your hero has transcended something and is open now to new possibilities?*

— *you can use this material in your story to convey your character's dreams or fears or aspirations?*

— *how music can suggest vivid details of a place?*

— *whether this material lends itself to poetry or prose? could you write a poem? a dream sequence for a story?*

Experiment 15
Descend a dream stairway[3]

Your guide will tell you these steps:

1. LIE DOWN, CLOSE your EYES, let tensions drain down from head to toe and out of your body.
2. VISUALIZE yourself when you were six years old.
3. REMEMBER a dream staircase at the back of the bedroom closet, and go down.
4. TRAVEL in a little boat, go ashore, look around.
5. Return and WRITE nonstop.

SCRIPT FOR YOUR GUIDE

Instruct experimenter(s) to put pad and pen close by.

1. *"GET COMFORTABLE lying on your back on the floor, and allow your eyes to close. Let the floor support your whole weight. . . . RELAX your forehead, and your face. . . . Let your jaw go limp . . .*

---

[3]This experiment was inspired by a procedure described by Masters and Houston in *Mind Games* (Delta, 1972).

and your neck. . . . [Move slowly down the body, suggesting that each part relax or go limp, right to the toes.]

2. *"Now your body is getting smaller, shrinking to the size it was when you were six years old. . . . You can see your hair . . . your arms and legs . . . chest . . . your young face. . . .*

3. *"Now you can remember a dream you used to have as a child. You're in bed. You get up and walk over to the closet, and find that there's a door at the back, and it opens. . . . There's a staircase of stone, and you're eager to go down it . . . you go step by step. . . . You look around . . . you hear water lapping. . . .*

4. *"At the bottom of the stairs, there's a little boat. You get in, . . . The boat rocks gently and begins moving toward some light ahead. . . . You go out through the opening, and you're in full sunlight, drifting downstream . . . the sun warms your face. . . . Look at the shoreline . . . smell the air, notice its coolness on your skin. . . . There's a meadow. . . . You float ashore, and get out of the boat . . . the grass touches your legs . . . it's beautiful . . . head for that big tree . . . run up to it, and sit down in its shade. . . . Glance around. . . . How do you feel? . . . Off in the distance you see something . . . what is it? . . . Do you want to go there? . . . Follow where you want to go. . . .* [Allow three minutes.]

5. *"Whenever you're ready, you can return to this room. You can sense your back on the floor. . . . Listen to the sounds in this room. . . . Allow your eyes to open slowly . . . and sit up. WRITE NONSTOP and tell what you saw and what happened from beginning to end."* [Optional: put on some soft flowing music in the background.]

Did you notice
> —*if each of your senses was engaged at some point?*
> —*how you can have access to "dream" material if you first relax in this way?*
> —*if there's an opening for a story here? a fairy tale? or could this material be a flashback?*

Experiment 16
Listen in—how do people talk?

1. MAKE A STUDY of how people talk.
   a. Watch TV with the sound off and notice postures, gestures, and facial expressions that accompany emotion. Can you guess what's being said and felt?
   b. Pick one person you meet today, and when he talks, particularly notice body language, the position of his arms, and facial expressions. Do you ever get a "double message" (when gestures or a look seem to say the opposite of the words coming out)? Notice tone of voice—how would you label it?
   c. Walk past public phones or sit in a coffee shop and eavesdrop: catch bits of conversation and record these in a notebook.

2. (For writing classes)

   THINK UP A CHARGED SITUATION (perhaps one in your story-to-be), and have two people spontaneously play out a scene. Just get one person to start talking, and the conversation will get going. As you observe, notice gestures, intonation, facial expression; become aware of how dialogue sounds when it rings true.

   Some sample scenes might be:
   a. After 30 years of marriage, she finds the nerve to ask him for a divorce. She begins, "John, it's time we had a little talk."
   b. She wants to break off the engagement but won't tell him why. "I have to go now, Peter."

3. MAKE A STUDY OF YOUR OWN BODY when you're afraid, angry, depressed, or excited. ACT OUT a "charged moment."

a. You're about to appear on live TV for the first time. Visualize yourself waiting to go on, and take that position. Scan your body from head to toe: How is your stomach? Fluttery? How about your breathing? Heartbeat? Pulse? Is one foot moving nervously?

b. You slam down the receiver of the telephone. You're furious! What do you do? What's the expression on your face? Jaw tight? Pound on something? Kick over something?

c. You're depressed and you can't stop worrying. How are you sitting? Slumped? Playing with a strand of hair? Moist around the eyes? A lump or knot in your throat?

4. Picture your main character TALKING TO SOMEONE about something that means a lot. Something's coming to a head, or something's about to be revealed!

Begin with a question such as X saying: "What have you got to tell me that's so important?" or: "Why have you come here?" Let each line prompt the next.

Did you notice
  —how body language can speak louder than words?
  —that a direct question forces a response?
  —how dramatic and fascinating the interaction between people can be? how dialogue holds your attention?
  —how you can verify, in your own body, appropriate postures and gestures for certain emotional states?

ESPECIALLY FOR STORY WRITERS

To create a main character, first do Experiment 9, p. 20. Then try these next four experiments as you grow a story from your experience now.

Experiment 17
Cook up a conflict

1. Sit by a window and picture your main character (X) sitting there. Today, right now, what is X's PROBLEM? On your scratch sheet, write a phrase describing X's problem at this moment.

   a. Write at the top of a page: X SAT BY THE WINDOW, LOOKING . . .
   b. Do a Relaxation Exercise: Close your eyes, relax your muscles from head to toe, follow ten breaths, listen to sounds, open your eyes.
   c. Write FREE-FLOW, using "X SAT . . ." as your springboard.

2. Write any scene in your story that shows X getting CLOSER to what X wants. Write any scene that shows X getting FARTHER away again from what X wants.
3. Write any scene in your story in which things "HEAT UP." What happens? What's at stake?
4. Write a scene in which X and someone else CLASH VERBALLY or have a hard time communicating. Make sure they interrupt each other. Or have one person reject everything the other person says. Use dialogue and details of tone of voice, posture, gesture, and movement ("dialogue tags").

For more on writing dialogue, see Experiment 16 ("Listen in—how do people talk?"), p. 38, and also "About Writing Dialogue," p. 54.

5. PLAN your SCENES. Make a LIST of possible scenes in your story just as if you were outlining a movie script. Which scenes are absolutely necessary to the story? Which are "filler" and not necessary? Rearrange the order of key scenes to create a sense of tension building—action "rising" to a climax.

Did you notice
   —what is driving your main character into these situations?
   —if there is a sense of tension building or action "rising" to a
      climactic turning point?
   —any surprises when you put your character in conflict with
      another?

If your story isn't quite coming onto the page, this next experiment may help you unlock a more interesting way to tell the story.

Experiment 18
Play with point of view[1]

1. If your story is in the first person ("I walked in"), rewrite the first page in THIRD PERSON ("She walked in").

Try this especially if your story is autobiographical.

2. If your story is written in the third person ("He always knew"), rewrite your first page in the FIRST PERSON ("I always knew").

Note that whoever tells the story will probably become the one the reader identifies with, the character that is "moved" by the action of the story.

3. Rewrite a scene of DIALOGUE TWO WAYS. First, write it from the point of view of one character writing in the first person ("I said"). Then write the same page, again in the first person, but from the point of view of the other character.

---

[1]Some of these suggestions were inspired by Janet Burroway's excellent book on the craft, *Writing Fiction*.

4. Choose a scene from your story and rewrite it from the point of view of a MINOR CHARACTER observing the main character.
5. Narrate the SAME EVENT (restaurant or party scene) from three different points of view. Which do you prefer?

For instance, X and Y go into a restaurant and meet Z. What happens? Write the scene, then rewrite it from Y's point of view, then from Z's point of view. You'll need to know about X, Y, and Z, their relationships, and the "unfinished business" among them.

6. Write a scene in which your main character is in an awkward or tense situation. Have him think one thing but say or do the opposite. (Put the character's thoughts in *italics*.)
7. Rewrite or write a scene so the observing narrator sees as a CAMERA would see, without interpretation or comment. For example, instead of saying how a character feels or what she thinks, describe only what a camera would see: posture, gesture, tone of voice, facial expression.

TIP: This approach is especially useful if your story gets bogged down in too much explanation. Remember: SHOW, DON'T EXPLAIN. Be a camera.

Did you notice
  —*a change in point of view is a change of story?*
  —*that trying out a different point of view can let new material into the story, material that may be more interesting?*
  —*you're less or more sure now about the point of view from which to tell the story?*
  —*when you use "I" to tell a story, the "I" becomes the character we most care about?*

Are you ready for the next step? The turning point comes when your character has a moment of realization, a "crisis" moment, or an epiphany. One way or another, something is discovered or resolved.

Experiment 19
Picture the turning point—what happens?

Try this experiment outdoors if possible, at the beach or by a river or stream.

1. Set up a blank page with some springboards for writing, like this:
   a. WRITE at the top your version of the following: *X sat by the river, waiting* . . .

In place of "X" put your character's name, or use "I" if writing in the first person. If you like, in place of "by the river," put your character wherever you want this "turning point" to occur (*in the hallway, at the beach, by the window*).

   b. Midway down the page, WRITE the phrase: *And then it happened*.
   c. Turn the page over, and near the bottom, place a large check mark in the margin.

NOTE: After the relaxation exercise, when you open your eyes, you'll write down your very first visual impression next to this CHECK MARK. Then you'll turn the paper over and begin writing nonstop.

2. Sit outdoors, or by a window, and do a RELAXATION EXERCISE: close your eyes, relax from head to toe, notice your breath moving in and out, and begin to listen to the sounds all around you.
3. Slowly OPEN your EYES, and next to the check mark on the page, DESCRIBE in a sentence the first thing you see.
4. IMAGINE your character is waiting here. Something is about to happen, a feeling is building, perhaps someone's coming any minute—and then it happens!

5. WRITE NONSTOP from the top of page one ("*X sat by the river, waiting . . .*"). Who comes? What's said? What happens next? What's resolved?
6. END the scene with a sensory detail—a version of the one you wrote next to the check mark. Let that detail leave your reader with a strong, single impression of what it all means.

Something's over now—or has just begun! Your last words might be "Two gulls glided above her and, with a cry, were gone."

Did you notice
—*how your imagination can take over once you open to a place and have the idea that something's about to happen there?*
—*that sensory details, rather than an explanation, can convey a powerful moment of experience?*
—*whether what you see depends on how you're feeling?*

Experiment 20
Let nature express your theme

Wait until your story has "gelled" into a rough draft before trying this one.

1. Sit OUTSIDE at a favorite, inspiring place.
2. Close your eyes. RELAX your muscles from head to toe. For two minutes, give all your attention to following your BREATHING while LISTENING to the sounds all around you as if nothing else matters but doing that. Open your eyes.
3. Describe, in one sentence, the very FIRST THING YOU SEE in the landscape.

   Example: *Bare branches and the winter sky seem lit from within.*

4. Turn so you face another vista, and REPEAT Steps 1–3.
5. (OPTIONAL) Face another vista, and do the experiment a third time.
6. Look at each sentence you've written as if it were the FINAL SENTENCE of a short story. In a word or two, what feeling does it leave you with? Hope? Resignation?

> Example: *Bare branches against the winter sky seem lit from within.*
> Feeling: Joy, renewed life

7. Lightly EDIT the sentence, which could be the final words of your story, so this IMAGE of nature, expressed in this particular RHYTHM of words, conveys a feeling of what the story means.

Did you notice
  —you discovered the theme of your story in the images that appeared on the page?
  —you clarified what final impression you want your readers to have?
  —that readers don't want you to tell them the theme or message of the story but want to feel something about the story and draw their own conclusions?
  —when you end with an image and a certain rhythm of words, you touch the feelings so the reader can experience the meaning of the story?
  —an image from nature makes a satisfying ending?

SHAPING WHAT COMES

You can build a story from the material you've generated doing Experiments 1 through 20. Here are some of the ways people take what they write free-flow and let it stimulate them to write more.

1. Read all you've written. UNDERLINE parts you like, especially sentences which suggest the GERM of a story.
2. Make up a MAIN CHARACTER (try Experiment 9, p. 20). Put that name instead of *I* in your writings.

45

Does any of it suggest a story yet? What could be his problem? Her situation? How is he feeling and why?

3. Combine material from different experiments. Insert the name of your main character What's about to happen to him?

   Don't worry about material which seems extra or doesn't fit. Put brackets [] around it.

4. NOW TRY TO WRITE JUST ONE PAGE, ANY PAGE, of your story.

   If several "scenes" suggest themselves and you don't know what to write first, start with the one you know you can write now—and *don't worry about your first sentence*, just get going. Later you'll sense where this material will fit. You may end up writing your opening last.

5. Are you at a point where you could put in some *dialogue*? Write nonstop one page or more. Who does she meet? Who could he talk to? What's the *conflict*?

6. When you have many sections of the story, put them in order. Which should come first? How do you want to introduce your character and the situation?

   Create a first draft of your story, using all the sections you've composed, weaving them together so something builds.

   Your story: it may take a shape all its own. If you're looking for a framework, though, here's a summary of one approach to organizing your material.

FIVE STEPS FOR STORY WRITERS

1. *Discover your main character.*
   Then start him out right in the middle of some activity or just before something is going to happen. With vivid sensory details, show him in action in a particular place.

2. *Place your character in conflict.*
   What's the situation? What's her problem? Is something about to occur? Who else is involved?

Conflict means opposing forces, potential fireworks. Have the situation "heat up" through

dialogue (include posture, gesture, tone of voice, facial expression), and

description (convey your character's state of mind by how he sees his surroundings).

Whenever possible, SHOW rather than explain. (Instead of "He was frightened," describe heartbeat, perspiration, breathing, or behavior.)

TENSION'S BUILDING. Conflict keeps things in motion, so the action "rises" to some intense moment.

3. *Move swiftly to the crisis*, turning point, or "moment of truth."

What happens? What's resolved? Which, if any, of the opposing forces triumphs? How is your character different now?

Stop once the action's over to avoid going on too long after the climax.

4. *Edit out parts that slow down the story.*
Where does the narrative drag? Does the action get lost in too many words? Is the lead-in too slow? Should you start on page two?

As an experiment, try cutting out every extra word you can find. Is it better? *Do events move swiftly to create a strong single impression?*

5. *Find a TITLE that's simple but evocative.*
Is there a key image or phrase from the story that could also have a symbolic or double meaning? Can the image suggest something of what happens to the main character?

For instance, "The Storm" can be both an inner and outer event. "Hills Like White Elephants" is what one character says in passing about the landscape—but the story is about a couple deciding about an abortion.

Thumb through your story and see if any phrases or images strike you. MAKE A LIST of words from the "world" of your story.

For instance, are you writing about an artist? Or about a base-ball player? Look up a key word (*art, baseball*) in the THESAURUS. If your story is about an artist, for instance, what are the names of artists' tools or materials? If about a baseball pitcher, what are the names of some pitches? Can any of those words convey a double meaning?

Let the title you choose mean more than one thing to your story. Is there a word or phrase that is appropriate in its *literal* meaning but also happens to say something about the *emotional* or psychological situation here as well?

Here are some EXAMPLES OF TITLES with double meanings:

"The Change-Up" (This name of a certain kind of baseball pitch also works in a story about a wounded pitcher's overcoming obstacles to pitch again.)

"Sisterhood" (This buzz word for women's solidarity has an ironic meaning in this story about the pernicious doings of a female street gang of hoods.)

"The *Consolation*" (In this story, there is a boat, ironically called the *Consolation*, which was left to an estranged son after the father dies.)

The simpler the title, the better. So find a title that's engaging, but not overdone. Type up your final draft. Good for you!

Part 4 (Becoming Your Own Best Editor) can help you tighten and sharpen your writing.

Rather than worrying about impressing a reader, please only yourself. Chances are if your writing rings true for you, someone else will be touched by it.

Would you like to know if your story does ring true? Ask a reader to use the Review Sheet below. CAUTION: Don't automatically change things just because you're told you should. Be true to your vision of the story. As you "grow your story," with each new draft, discover what that truth really is and how to get it on the page.

REVIEW SHEET FOR STORIES

1. Does the first page hold your interest and make you want to read on? If not, where do you lose interest? What does THE OPENING need?

2. Who is the main CHARACTER (X) and what's his predicament?

   a. What does X want? (For both his "inner" and "outer" world.)
   b. What stands in X's way? (In both his "inner" and "outer" world.)
   c. What unfinished emotional business is driving this character?
   d. What would help you care more about X?
   e. What would make X more believable, more like a real person?

3. What is the CONFLICT? Where, if anywhere, do you lose the sense of something building?

   Place a QUESTION MARK next to stray passages that slow the pace or seem beside the point. Where, if anywhere, does the story BOG DOWN for you? Where, if anywhere, doesn't it RING TRUE?

4. When the story ends, what strong impressions are you left with? What is this story really about? Is the ENDING satisfying? What would make the ending better?

5. What does this writer DO WELL?

   Place a CHECK MARK next to sentences which are WELL-PUT.

6. What does this story MOST NEED now?

   If you can, write two specific SUGGESTIONS for improving this story.

7. OTHER COMMENTS?

WRITING AN AUTOBIOGRAPHICAL ESSAY
OR ORAL HISTORY

You've had a powerful experience that taught you something. Perhaps it's come out in your free-flow writing. You wonder whether it might become the germ of an article or essay.

What's your purpose in writing the piece? Do you want to:

—entertain?

—inform?

—comment on human nature?

—relive, explore, or understand something?

—instruct yourself through your writing?

Fine! When you speak from experience, you create a feeling of shared intimacy. Be confident that when you write in vivid detail what you've lived, it'll reach someone who's felt the same thing.

Showing what happened is not reserved for fiction alone. A pertinent incident or conversation will liven up and make a strong point in any essay. You can follow the chronological order of events as they happened, or begin just before a moment of realization. Try flashing back or forward in time. Dialogue will make your writing come alive.

Experiment 21
Tell about life

A death, a birth, a loss, a discovery, a wonderful friend, an adventure, a first love . . . the unexpected, the unexplainable, the joy of being alive, another level breaking through. . . . These powerful moments we share connect us all.

Version 1: An intense moment of your life

1. Start a LIST of the most intense moments of your life, ones that stand out most vividly in memory. Add to this list for a day or two.

If you keep a JOURNAL or diary, "mine" it for moments to put on your list.

2. Do a RELAXATION EXERCISES (p. 13) to clear a space for a fresh impulse. Then write FREE-FLOW for ten minutes, beginning "I'LL NEVER FORGET THE TIME . . ."

3. Like a fiction writer, just tell the STORY. Be as HONEST and plain-speaking as you can. Stick to one intense experience, and begin it *just before* the moment of greatest emotional impact.

Stay with exactly what happened without explanation. Every scene adds to a sense of action rising to a climactic moment. Just show us what happened as simply as you can. Be sincere with yourself and don't exaggerate or interpret. Don't load us with background—trust that we'll understand. Stick with the action!

4. Conclude at the moment of GREATEST EMOTIONAL IMPACT.

To avoid being anticlimatic, don't say what happened afterward or how you felt. Let the action of the story, and how it ends, leave us with a tug on the spirit.

5. (OPTIONAL) Let others read or hear your story. Read it aloud to a group of people.

Version 2: An oral history: An intense moment of someone else's life

There's someone you know who has many great stories to tell. It could be a grandparent, a parent, a visiting relative, a neighbor, a senior citizen, a retired person, the town historian. Experience the flavor of another time and place the struggles of another human being when the world was "different:" take down an "oral history."

1. Write down a LIST of questions you can use to get the person to begin talking about her life.
2. INTERVIEW the person in a comfortable setting, preferably her own home. Ask if you can use a small cassette player to TAPE what's said. Then you won't feel you have to write and can just LISTEN.
3. Try to LISTEN as if you are receiving sound with the whole of your body.

Where does the person's voice resonate in your body? In the head? In the abdomen? Be aware of your seat on the chair. If you can, try to see yourself there, sitting like that, listening. When you become more aware of your body sitting there, it may help you receive a fresh impression.

4. WRITE FREE-FLOW in any order, including everything that comes up. Do this at home or in a nearby coffee shop as soon after the interview as possible.

Keep a notepad or tape recorder with you so that later, when more details come to you, or ideas for how to begin your essay or article, you record them.

5. Go back for ANOTHER SESSION on another day—you'll get a different story! Tape it; listen with awareness; later, write free-flow.
6. Write the article or essay. QUOTE THE PERSON telling the most exciting or moving moments.
   a. Begin with a brief description of the person in the setting in which you interviewed her. Use quotations (put in quotation marks) so the person tells her own story. Insert your comments briefly when you feel you need to vary the pace of the essay or shift gears to another incident.
   b. End with a "clincher": the part of the story that most grabbed you when you first heard it! Stop there.

c. Edit out the parts that are "filler": like a fiction writer, create a sense of action rising to a moment of realization. SHOW what's exciting; summarize the rest in a phrase.

OPTIONAL: Read "oral histories" at the library. Find articles in which people are interviewed and tell about their life. See how other writers handle this material and present it in an engaging way.

Version 3: Life moments which teach us

1. What LESSON about life, people, or yourself did you learn from an intense moment you recall? SAY out loud that lesson in a sentence. Write it down. You may want to use that as your final sentence—or as your opening.
2. ILLUSTRATE that lesson with an incident which you narrate as if it were a short story.
3. CONCLUDE at the moment of greatest impact. How did you feel at that moment of realization? What has that moment taught you? Tell us simply. No need to explain or embellish: say it in plain English.

Did you notice
—a sense of well-being once you told your story?
—your surprise when others hearing your story tell you that the same thing happened to them?
—when you write honestly about your experience, a tone of voice comes through which touches others?

Whether you want to do a story or an essay, think about it, plan, but START WRITING—even a page! More ideas will come *while* you're putting words on paper. If you get stuck, find any part that you could write now: there's usually some description or dialogue you can get into. Build momentum by writing nonstop again and again.

ABOUT WRITING DIALOGUE

"Oh, please. . . ."

"Forget it!"

What's happened between these two? Want to find out? Give the speakers names, and write the rest of the conversation.

Dialogue is easy to take in, and engaging. Even an ordinary report can be enlivened by quoting. A person's voice has a directness and immediacy that says a lot about a situation.

For dialogue that rings true, try the following, where appropriate. Then read out loud what you wrote.

1. Use contractions (*I've, don't, you've*).
2. Try slang expressions that fit the age and upbringing of your character.
3. Use direct questions, with question marks, to provoke a response.
4. Be sure to indicate who's speaking (so there are no disembodied voices).

   a. Begin a new paragraph (indent five spaces) each time the speaker changes.

      If only two people are talking, see if it's clear who's speaking without naming the person (for a few lines at least).

   b. Have the person talk. Then within the same paragraph, as your **"dialogue tag"** to let us know who just spoke, follow with a sentence indicating the speaker's posture or movement, such as:

      "Won't you sit down just for a minute?" Sandra poured out two cups of coffee.

Showing posture or gesture in the same paragraph as the quotation indicates who's speaking without having to write "he said."

5. Take care not to replace "said" with elegant variations which, if used with every quotation, would call attention to themselves ("she chortled," "he pleaded," "he bellowed"). Don't overdo your dialogue tags! The simpler, the better.
6. Look through an anthology of short stories. Use any page of dialogue as a MODEL for setting up your own. How does the writer achieve a balance between speech and action?

In the story below, respectable farmer Peter goes a little crazy when his wife dies; he begins to reveal embarrassing secrets to his neighbor Ed. Notice how dialogue and description strike a balance: "he said" is hardly used, but you know who's talking and can see him move and gesture. And you want to read on!

> . . . Ed's hand went out toward the bromide bottle, but Peter shook his head.
> "No need to give me anything, Ed. I guess the doctor slugged me pretty hard, didn't he? I feel all right now, only a little dopey."
> "If you'll just take one of these, you'll get some sleep."
> "I don't want to sleep." He fingered his draggled beard and then stood up. "I'll go out and wash my face, then I'll feel better."
> Ed heard him running water in the kitchen. In a moment he came back into the living-room, still drying his face on a towel. Peter was smiling curiously. It was an expression Ed had never seen on him before, a quizzical, wondering smile. "I guess I kind of broke loose when she died, didn't I?" Peter said.
> "Well—yes, you carried on some."
> "It seemed like something snapped inside of me," Peter explained. "Something like a suspender strap. . . ."
>
> (from John Steinbeck's
> "The Harness")

Use this, or any dialogue you read, as a model for setting up the conversation you write.

Look over the dialogue and note if it moves the story forward. Does something "heat up"? Is anything revealed?

ABOUT WRITING HUMOR AND PARODIES

Reading humor can get you into the mood for writing it. As you read, what does the author do with the text that makes you laugh?

For instance, look through *It Was a Dark and Stormy Night*, a book of "the funniest opening sentences from the worst novels never written," compiled by Scott Rice from contest entries. Then try any of the suggestions below.

Whatever you try, have fun with it! Don't criticize while you're writing: you can edit later. Right now, allow yourself the time to let your own wry sense of humor become active and show itself on the page.

Experiment 22
Humor yourself

1. Write a PARODY of a certain GENRE (such as pulp romance, gothic romance, spy novel, historical fiction, horror story, children's book, whodunit).

   a. Choose your MODEL, typical of the kind of fiction you want to parody. It could be fiction you love—or hate—to read. Browse at the library or in the bookstore, or see what's on your shelf.

   b. Make a LIST of words, settings, and situations typical of this type of fiction. Have you chosen a highly researched historical novel loaded with obscure words no one knows (what's a *drindle sac*?)? Or an espionage thriller with fourteen different spies per chapter? Or do you favor a gothic romance with that scary old castle on the hill and the bosomy damsel in distress? What are the clichés of this genre?

   c. Give your characters NAMES that connote STEREOTYPES (e.g. "Victor Machete" in a macho pulp romance) or names that OVERDO ("Wittle Bitty Bunny Boopsy" in a sappy toddler's book).

d. EXAGGERATE typical sentences in your MODEL. Lay it on thick with too many flowery adjectives, overly long sentences, obvious stereotypes, mixed metaphors, and clichés—so we know you're writing tongue-in-cheek!

(Pulp romance) *The enormous floor-to-ceiling windows of the Starlight Room were filled with a breath-taking patchwork of runway markers and warning flashers, quiescent now but swept into frenzied motion whenever a plane took off. But Victor had eyes only for Carla. How he longed to crush her against his feverish chest, to press that Jell-O softness until it spread all through him, soothing away the anvil weight of the day. . . .*

2. LIST three IRRITATING situations or BEHAVIOR forms. Write sarcastically about what gripes you, what you observe, and what you know best. Give telling details, and exaggerate for humorous effect.

> EXAMPLES: driving cars
> waiting in line
> shopping at the supermarket
> entertaining the in-laws
> living with someone who has annoying habits

3. SUBSTITUTE the names of FAMOUS PEOPLE (or a famous couple) for the names of the characters in the parody you wrote in step 1.

For more on humor, try writing a "humorous how-to" (Exp. 26). See also the Humor Options on pp. 68–69.

Did you notice
—*that writing something funny is not as hard as you thought?*
—*that once you've got a takeoff point and get in a certain frame of mind, funny things can just pop up?*
—*when you have fun with the writing, your reader will, too?*

Chapter 3

Explaining Something

How should you explore your subject?
You can ask yourself a question, or a series of questions, about it. Try interviewing people. You might read what others have written.

Here are some additional ways to help you discover your slant.

The Grafitti Game, for instance, is a great technique for getting into any area of discussion. Put a "hot issue," in a word or phrase, on a blackboard, and watch each person respond to it with another word or phrase that gives her slant. Soon someone reacts to that, and puts up another phrase. Watch your "group poster poem" grow, and with it, a sense of shared creativity.

Experiment 23
Play the Graffiti Game

Two or twenty can play. The idea is to make something together with words and phrases, and watch your creation unfold. You can use a blackboard and chalk (white or colors). Or set up a large white poster or polymer board on a chair or easel, and have some colored Magic Markers ready. Or simply do this with one or two others writing in turn on a large pad.

Version 1: Write a "group poster poem"

1. To warm up, have everyone write free-flow for five minutes. "NOW I'M SITTING HERE AND." Go!
2. Have everyone read over his writing, and circle or underline interesting phrases.
3. On the poster or board, write: "NOW." Encourage someone to go up and add a phrase anywhere on the board in any kind of lettering. Encourage another person to add to it. Be patient until things get moving, and watch each addition to the group poem. When the space is covered, suggest that someone finish it. Enjoy what you've made together! Read it aloud.

Version 2: Explore any subject, concept, or word

1. Put a word or phrase on the board which will be the "theme" or "subject" of exploration.

   (One group wanted to investigate attitudes about men and women. To begin, a person wrote HE on the right half and SHE on the left half of the board.)

2. Encourage participants to write words or phrases anywhere on the empty space, noting each person's addition before putting up another. When you feel you've explored all the angles, suggest that someone complete the group poster poem.

Version 3. Use different kinds of music or sound effects

1. Select in advance a few different kinds of *instrumental* music, and together do one group poster poem to each piece.

   (Try a poem to Stockhausen's "Kontake" and see what electronic music suggests to the participants. Do another poster poem to a lilting classical piece. Or to the roar of the ocean.)

2. Erase the board or start with a clean sheet each time you complete a poster poem and change the music. Explore the various themes different sounds suggest.

Did you notice
   —how words generate more phrases and ideas?
   —anything revealing about people's attitudes or beliefs?
   —interesting juxtapositions, or anything startling or clever?
   did some subjects call forth only stock and clichéd responses?
   —how music and free-flow writing stimulate writing?
   —a feeling of satisfaction, pride, or closeness develop in the group? or, just the opposite?

Experiment 24
Find sensory specifics to illustrate ideas

---

1. If your subject is an abstract noun such as *shame, freedom, boredom,* or *success,* write it at the left side of a blackboard, posterboard, or pad. Write these headings across the top:

   looks like?   tastes like?
   sounds like?   feels like to touch?
   smells like?

2. By yourself, or with others, fill in those columns. What does boredom look like? "A hundred tract houses." What does boredom sound like? "A dripping faucet." Be as specific as you can. List *four* concrete sensory details for *each* heading.
3. Don't write down a word or phrase unless it's more specific than your original "idea" noun. That is, don't accept responses like *tedium* or *monotony* for "What does boredom look like?"

60

Ask, "What does monotony look like?" until you get some specific detail you can perceive with your senses.

4. For more practice, erase the board or take a clean sheet, and write another abstract word on it. Discover some new ways to describe some old feelings.

Did you notice

—*that you can find vivid sensory equivalents for nearly any "idea" word?*

—*that the more you try to find such specifics, the more occur to you?*

—*if it's easier to find sights and sounds than textures, tastes, or smells? that it is possible to find details which engage all the senses?*

Experiment 25
Contrast then and now

Version 1: Explore your attitudes about the sexes

1. Write across the top of a page: "WHEN I WAS YOUNGER, I." Turn the page over and write across the top "I REMEMBER ONE TIME." Across the top of the third sheet write: "NOW I." You can try this yourself, or have a friend direct you.[1]

2. Open with your relaxation exercise (p. 13) done lying down.

3. PICTURE yourself as you were in junior high, at a school dance. What are you wearing? Look around. What are you feeling about the others there? Boys? Girls? Watch your movements as the scene unfolds. . . . Recall and return to an instant when you experienced something about the sexes for the first time. What happens? How do you feel? . . .

---

[1] NOTE TO YOUR GUIDE: Speak quietly, don't hurry, as you give the steps of the Relaxation Exercise; then give steps three and four below. Pause for a minute before giving step four.

4. Open your eyes, pick up your pen, and WRITE NONSTOP, completing the sentence. Do it quickly. When you turn the page and come to a new heading, go with that and keep your pen moving. Cover all three pages with words.

5. To supplement this material, INTERVIEW PEOPLE:

   a. TALK with your mother or father, asking, "What advice did you used to give me about (boys) (girls) (men) (women)?"
   b. TALK with a childhood pal or best friend. RECALL how you each felt about the opposite sex: can you remember an earlier incident or conversation? Did you have a stereotyped image of what men or women were like?
   c. WRITE FREELY NONSTOP: "When I was young, boys were. . . ." Or "When I was young, girls were. . . ." Let specific incidents from your experience make the writing come alive.

Here's a sample, from Anne Roiphe's "Confessions of a Female Chauvinist Sow." When she was younger, she whole-heartedly believed the stereotyped view of boys:

> Boys were fickle and likely to be unkind; my mother and I knew that, as surely as we knew they tried to make you do things in the dark they wouldn't respect you for afterwards, and in fact would spread the word and spoil your rep. Boys like to be flattered; if you made them feel important they would eat out of your hand. So talk to them about their interests, don't alarm them with displays of intelligence. . . . Altogether—without anyone directly coming out and saying so—I gathered that men were sexy, powerful, very interesting, but not very nice, not very moral, humane and tender, like us. . . .

   d. To explore this area more deeply, try Experiment 28.

Version 2: Explore your ambitions

1. Write across the top of the page: "WHEN I WAS YOUNGER, I WANTED." Write across the top of the other side "NOW I WANT."

2. Lie down, and open with your relaxation exercise (p. 13).
3. PICTURE yourself at graduation. A classmate asks you, "So, what do you want to do with your life?" What do you tell her?
4. Open your eyes, pick up your pen, and write nonstop completing the sentence on the first page. When you come to the next heading, keep the pen moving.
5. TALK with parents or relatives, asking, "When I was young, what did you think I'd turn out to be?"

Did you notice
   —any surprises in what you wrote or what others said to you?
   —how earlier experiences affected your attitudes?
   —whether your views have changed, and in what ways?
   —that sometimes you don't know what you think until you see what you say on paper?
   —that writing can help you understand more clearly what you really feel?

Experiment 26
Write a humorous "how-to"

Magazines constantly print advice from experts about how to do things like lose weight or make money. In this unlikely "how-to" piece, pretend to give "serious" advice about how to do something that no one wants to do.

NOTE TO TEACHERS: This makes a great first assignment for composition students. It makes writing enjoyable and brings out one's natural voice.

Version 1: To entertain

1. Make up a TITLE for your essay. To do this, first make a list of several possible subjects such as FAMILY, JOB, MONEY, LOVE,

SCHOOL, SIBLINGS, PARENTS, PARTIES, SPORTS, VACA-
TIONS. (To really get going, brainstorm titles in a small peer
group.)

SAMPLE TITLES

How to Be a Health Hazard
How to Waste a Minute
How to Throw a Terrible Party
How to Drive Your English Teacher Crazy

2. Write an OPENING PARAGRAPH in which you show why
your reader would want to learn to do what you suggest.
Remember: your tone is mock-serious (tongue-in-cheek). For
instance, ask your reader questions:

SAMPLE OPENINGS

*Does everyone always end up at your place for parties? Are you
sick of shoveling your way through tons of old pizza and soda
cans the morning after? Follow these steps and your friends will
never ask to party at your house again!*

*Is your English teacher getting on your nerves? Tired of the
same old what-I-did-on-my-summer-vacation assignments? Add
some excitement to this semester: drive the teacher crazy! Here's
how.*

3. Write a SERIES OF STEPS the reader can take to learn how to
"do" whatever you're explaining. (You can list and number the
steps if you like.) Write COMMANDS (do this, try that).

SAMPLE STEPS
from "How to Drive Your English Teacher Crazy"

*First, wear a different wig every day of the week and sit in a
different seat . . .*

*Second, never punctuation and not complete sentences cannot
read it even hard to do but you can as many errors grammar got
the idea?*

4. Put in SPECIFICS. Exaggerate! Don't put in the expected—surprise the reader with your unlikely combinations of vivid specifics.

INSTEAD OF GENERALIZATIONS	PUT IN SPECIFICS
Tired of being slim? Want to change your look quickly? Eat a lot of fattening food each day.	*Tired of being slim? Eat this yummy "super sundae" every morning: six quarts of Rocky Road ice cream topped with sausage, mozzarella cheese, chicken fat and marshmallow.*

5. End with a CLINCHER—the final, most outrageous step. Or sum up the benefits of your advice—how it's worked for you and can work for your reader, too.

Did you notice
—*that finding a title you like can unlock the whole piece for you?*
—*how piling on specifics brings a smile?*
—*that funny things occur to you to write once you're in motion?*

Version 2: To inform
Do a straightforward "How-To."

1. Answer the question: "What do I know how to do that someone else would want to know how to do?" Decide what process you'll describe.
2. Write at the top of a page: "HOW TO (*your subject*)." Below, list step 1, step 2, step 3. . . .
3. TALK out each step, then write it down just that way.

Assume your reader knows nothing about this procedure.
—Is each step clear? Small enough? Do you need to add another step just to help her follow more easily?
—Are there terms your reader might not know? Explain them.

—Any pitfalls she might encounter? Warn against common mistakes.

4. READ ALOUD to someone just to be sure you've got all the steps, with no gaps, or confusing parts. Ask your listener to tell you which part she needs to hear again.

5. WRITE an introductory sentence or two, perhaps opening with an ANECDOTE that tells what it was like the first time you tried to make a soufflé, develop a photo, repair fiberglass.

Did you notice
  —how clear you have to be about a process before telling others?
   that explaining it made it clearer to you?
  —anything new about something you do automatically?
  —if you kept to "one step, one sentence?"

███████

Experiment 27
Research a burning question

1. Do an Interests Inventory.

   You want to become an expert on a subject that really interests you. FILL IN this sheet:

   What do I want to know more about?
   1.
   2.
   3.

2. CHOOSE the most intriguing item, and write free-flow a few sentences, answering:
   What about it? What do I want to understand?
   What could I find out?

3. Ask yourself the question you'll want to answer.[2] Write it down on an index card.

---

[2] Such as, How did writing begin? What are the origins of golf? What are man's possibilities for development? Where does electricity come from and where does it go? What's a quasar?

—How (Who) (What) (Where) (Why) (When) _____
_____ ?

4. Go on a TREASURE HUNT at the library to gather material that'll make you an expert on this subject. Don't stop until you have your answer. Look at your index card often so you're clear about just what you need (and what you don't).

   —Underline key words in your question, to guide you through card catalogues. What's your SUBJECT?
   —Check subject cards (arranged alphabetically) in the card catalogue, and write down the names and call numbers of BOOKS which might have what you need.
   —Check subject entries (also arranged alphabetically) in the *Reader's Guide to Periodical Literature* (this year's, or whatever year when articles might have been written about your subject), and copy down the names and volume and page for MAGAZINES which might contain what you need.
   —Ask the librarian if you're not sure where to look for these books and magazines.
   —Glance at your card again, then check through the INDEX at the back of each book. Photocopy pages with material you need, or make notes. Be sure to write down the book, author, publisher, city of publication, year of publication, and page numbers.
   —Skim or photocopy appropriate magazine articles. Be sure to write down publishing information (titles, author, publication, volume, date, page) for each source you use.

5. Read over your notes, underline highlights. Do you have your answer yet? Find out by trying some free-flow writing. Do Experiment 48. Go on to Experiment 49 to come up with your first draft. If you need suggestions for ways to shape your essay, see below.

Did you notice
   —*there's more to the answer than you thought?*
   —*your question got more specific as you researched it?*
   —*it's useful to work on something you really care to know about?*

—anything exciting in your exploration which leads to other questions you might want to answer?

SHAPING WHAT COMES

SIX WAYS TO EXPLAIN

Explaining something means telling what's what. You elaborate on the causes, results, stages, steps, reasons, types, relationships.

Here's a brief description of different ways to present the facts.

1. *Illustrate* with examples: show what something is.

   Sensory specifics help ideas come alive. After writing an opening which gives your slant on a topic, illustrate your point with a series of telling examples. Save the "clincher" for last.

2. *Define:* tell what something is.

   Some essays first define key terms so your reader knows just how you're using an important word. A dictionary can help. Quote part of the entry as a way to introduce your subject.

   HUMOR OPTION ONE: Write a page from a mock catalogue of college courses. Brainstorm a list of serious-sounding titles for flimsy or bizarre courses. Then "define" each course and "illustrate" with specifics (such featured activities, made-up names of textbooks). Use a real college catalogue as your model. Write up the descriptions as if you were serious.

   Or, do a parody of any organization's daily schedule of activities. This could be a Camp Schedule or a day in the life at Club Dread. Next to the time, give the title of the activity. Then define and illustrate with outrageous specifics.

3. *Discover the parts* of a whole: "Three are three kinds of . . ."

   You researched a burning question and discovered the different aspects or parts of your subject, their relationship to each other and to the whole. You sort out, and arrange: what kinds or types exist? (Later you may want to contrast categories and illustrate with specifics.)

HUMOR OPTION TWO: Write a humorous version of "There are three kinds of . . ." Brainstorm a list of possible ways to complete that sentence until you find one which brings a mischievous smile. Make up a funny name for each category, and get going with a sentence like this:

There are three kinds of freshmen in my English class: Mr. Baseball Cap, Ms. Serious Grades, and Mr. Business Major.

4. *Compare or contrast* (show what something is or is not like).

List qualities or characteristics shared by X and Y: these are your bases of comparison. For instance, both plants X and Y have roots; both flower, and need light. Roots, flowers, light: items 1, 2, and 3 you'll compare in detail for X and Y. Or contrast them: X and Y both have roots, *but* X's roots are shorter; both flower, *but* Y rarely yields fruits; they both need light, *but* Y thrives in the shade. You've shown how two things are like and different. A fair comparison or contrast gives equal attention to X and Y, looking at item 1 for each, item 2, then item 3. See Experiment 43 (p. 132).

5. *Show how:* steps in a process.

Demonstrate how to do or how we do something by breaking the process into steps small enough so a reader can follow. Give examples. If the process is complex, take a small part at a time, and sort out the main steps. Write "first," "second," "next."

6. *Show why:* causes and effects, problems and solutions.

Your burning question may have led to discoveries about why and how something happened. You researched an event and traced its causes. Decide whether to move from causes to effects, or work back from effects to causes: which would be the stronger way to present your material? (Also, remember that just because something happened before something else, the first didn't necessarily *cause* the second.) Look for several causes, both immediate and remote. Did event A *result* in event B?

If a particular problem interests you, consider it as an "effect" and discover its causes. They may lead you to possible solutions. Ask yourself, why did this happen and what can be done? Weigh the advantages and disadvantages (make lists) of possible solutions, so you can decide on the best answer. In your essay, state the problem, what brought it about, and suggest ways to deal with it. End on that strong note.

Experiments in the next chapter show how you can persuade your reader.

Chapter 4

Convincing Someone

What makes us listen to one person and not another? Can you remember the last time someone convinced you of something? What did it take?

We want to trust the person speaking. Does he sound intelligent, fair, and reasonable? We'd like to respect the writer and feel that he respects us.

What would keep a reader from sharing your views, accepting your reasoning, and taking the action you suggest? Perhaps she doesn't understand the ideas you're explaining: are you clear? Or, she doesn't like what's coming through: are you browbeating or talking down to your reader? Or, she doesn't think you're justified in saying what you do: have you presented enough evidence to validate your opinion?

Convincing someone takes the right balance of logic and emotion. If the reader feels you're humane, honest, and sincerely searching for truth, she may go along with you. But first, do you believe what you're saying, and has it come out on the page as you'd like?

Experiment 28
Give your views about men and women today

Try this first part[1] with others to get an impression of today's attitudes about *men* and *women*.

1. DIVIDE into small groups, all-male, all-female and mixed. Each group has to come up with a single LIST of ten characteristics of the ideal man, ranked from most important to least important. Make the most important number 1.
2. Have each group write "the ideal *woman* is. . . ." List ten qualities, ranked from most important (number 1) to least important (number 5). Then do a list for "the ideal *man*."
3. Collect the lists, and have someone read them randomly. After each list is read, can you guess whether it characterizes a woman or man? Was it written by a men's or women's group? Any sex-typing or stereotyping?

Continue to explore on your own:

1. SEND OUT A QUESTIONNAIRE, or INTERVIEW people you know, young and old. Ask each to list the characteristics of an ideal man and then of an ideal woman, ranked from most important to least important. Help them by beginning, "A man should be . . ." and "A woman should be. . . ."
2. Freely write, nonstop, your impressions from these interviews. What strikes you?
3. CLIP a few ADS from magazines which depict this society's view of the ideal man or woman. Freely WRITE a page debunking what you consider the commonly held view of men

---

[1] Inspired by an activity suggested by Janaro and Gearhart, *Human Worth* (New York: Holt, Rinehart, and Winston, Inc., 1973), p. 572.

or women today. (You can make a COLLAGE of these pictures to accompany your essay or article.)

4. Write an essay exploring what makes for a healthy relationship. Take off from a quotation you've read that hits the mark, or write freely from one of these:

". . . it is incongruous with the nature of love
to try to reduce the loved person to 'an item
in one's personal world,' or to try to make
him comply with one's demands, or to try to
exert power over him in whatever way."

(Andras Angyal, 1951)[1]

"and the great renewal of the world will
perhaps consist in this, that man and maid,
freed of all false feelings and reluctances,
will seek each other not as opposites, but
as brother and sister, as neighbors, and will
come together *as human beings*. . . ."

(Rainer Maria Rilke, 1903)[2]

"In front of every human being, I should support him, understand him, be free of him and respect his freedom, and remember what we have in common; yes, in front of *all* others. But I know I am not capable. Let me at least try to be like that in front of you, because you are my friend, because you prepared the way for me and made the task easier for me. So in your presence at any rate I should not allow myself any weakness; all our meetings should be sacred moments."

(René Daumal, 1953)[3]

Did you notice
—anything surprising about people's attitudes?

---

[1] Andras Angyal, "A theoretical model for personality studies," *Journal of Personality*, Vol. 20, Sept. 1951.
[2] Rainer Maria Rilke, *Letters to a Young Poet* (New York, 1963) 38–39.
[3] René Daumal, *Chaque fois que l'aube paraît* (Paris, 1953). Translated from the French.

—something new about your own?
—whether we're all influenced by stereotypes? to what degree?

Experiment 29
Freely write your gripe

Version 1: Minor gripes

1. Write across the top of your pad: "WHAT REALLY GETS ME MAD?" Turn the page over and write at the top: "WHAT CAN WE DO ABOUT IT?"
2. Write nonstop, talking on paper as fast as you can. If more than one thing occurs to you, fine. Write your BIGGEST GRIPE(S).
3. Decide what TONE you'll use and who your AUDIENCE is. Picture your reader. Are you writing a satiric piece to amuse your peers? A persuasive piece to convince a particular group?
4. Write a draft, and then TRY OUT your material on a few people. Read aloud, so you hear where you need to revise. Ask listeners to tell you which parts convince them.

Did you notice
—where you sound really sure in your writing?
—where things "heat up" because you've tapped a strong feeling?
—if others share your gripe and enjoy hearing it expressed so fervently?
—if the tone is right for getting readers to respond in the way you want?

Version 2: Major problems and issues

We all have strong feelings about social issues and environmental problems facing us. How to make people aware of a serious problem in a fresh way? You want to appeal to reason, but more important, you want to appeal to the emotions of the reader.

1. Pose on paper the specific QUESTIONS you want to explore. Then do your research and fieldwork as thoroughly as possible. Take careful notes.
2. To open your article or essay, paint a picture in IMAGES or tell a STORY to dramatize the problem.

As John Muir observed, "Dry words and dry facts will not fire hearts." Generalizing, or writing too much in the abstract about a problem distances your reader from your subject. However, when you open with the struggles of one or two persons, or present vivid specifics, you make the issue more immediate and personal for the reader. For instance, if you're writing in support of doctor-assisted suicide, you might open with a "case" or two, one or two people's situations (use first names) the reader can identify with. If you're writing about homelessness, visit a shelter and narrate what happens.

3. Write with COMPASSIONATE OBJECTIVITY.

Consistently control your tone to sound as fair-minded as possible. Your humane tone can touch another human being. For example, if you're writing about depletion of the ozone layer, begin with a poetic description which makes us feel anew the beauty of the earth so that, like you, we respond with alarm at this picture of what may happen.

Never scold the reader. Avoid preaching or railing about a subject. Avoid exaggerating in any way for fear your reader will discount what you say as biased.

4. If necessary, DEFINE key words (*What are CFC's?*) or include a brief history the reader may not know. For example, if appropriate, give the current status (legal, scientific, environmental) of the situation.

5. Bring in key STATISTICS if pertinent. Numbers can shock the reader into paying attention while adding a quality of objectivity to your account.
6. Indicate the DIRECTION we need to go, or pose a question which readers then answer for themselves.
7. READ ALOUD your piece to a few people. Can you hear, in reading aloud, where the writing is less effective—where it sounds exaggerated or like propaganda, and needs to be revised? Can your listener tell you which parts work well and which parts do not?
8. End your piece with a final image or sentence which leaves the reader with a TUG ON THE SPIRIT.

A NOTE ON ADVOCACY JOURNALISM: Advocacy writing *can* make a difference. For example, environmentalist Rachel Carson, working alone, expressed her research findings in *Silent Spring*, a book which dramatically changed policies and viewpoints. Here's her simple advice to writers: "Do your homework. Speak good English. And care a lot."

Did you notice
—*how powerful the writing becomes when you talk about specific people rather than in generalizations?*
—*how vivid examples and a compassionate tone keep your reader involved?*
—*if you search, you can find a way to leave the reader with a tug on the spirit?*

SHAPING WHAT COMES

What do you say and how do you say it? No matter how impressive your facts, if you sound like a crank when you present them, you'll lose your reader.

Reading out loud helps you hear what's coming through. Listen to your opening sentence: if you read that, how would you respond? Would you go on?

You want to sound reasonable, fair, intelligent, sincere, and straightforward. You don't want to bore, irritate, or confuse. If you were talking with someone, and could see her response as you spoke, you'd know you were going on too long. Are you as effective on paper as you are in person? You can be!

Listen for tone of voice. Consider your reader's interests, and speak to them, if only to keep her reading so you have the chance to make your case.

Here are some patterns for organizing your material:

1. Move from a simple, familiar idea to a more complex one. (Choose an example or a comparison from ordinary life that your reader understands.)
2. Go from the most easily proven point (the most readily acceptable) to the least (especially if what you propose is threatening or unusual).
3. Use examples to support your view, moving from least to most convincing. Build a strong case, and clinch it.

To sum up, when you're shaping what comes, try this:

1. Picture your reader and step into her shoes. Now, what would convince you?
2. Write as you speak, in your natural voice.
3. Develop one aspect in a paragraph, then move on.
4. Save the clincher for last.
5. Try out this writing on others, asking what tone comes through. Any strong reactions to certain parts? Any jargon, or confusing places? (Try Experiment 50.)

Have you discovered an approach, a voice, or a style that works for you?

Chapter 5

Especially for Business Writers

What's the secret of business writing that succeeds? Make it easy to understand! Get to the point, supply specifics and benefits, suggest the next step. Everyday words expressed in a pleasant, respectful manner get the response you want.

But how to get going? You're faced with a writing task. You need to push the start button. Instead of procrastinating, try this startup sheet.

Experiment 30
Get going with this startup sheet

Follow the PQR Formula: Purpose, Question, Response. (Short version: do only Steps 1, 2, and 3.)

1. State for yourself your PURPOSE. Picture your reader (your AUDIENCE). On your scratch pad, fill in these specifics:

   My purpose is to get (whom?) to (do what exactly?)

2. Write at the top of a page the QUESTION you'll answer:

   What do I need to tell (whom?) about (my topic?)?

   Example: *What do I need to tell Mr. Jones about the new marketing plan?*

3. RESPOND by talking on paper for five minutes *without stopping* and *without criticizing* what comes.
4. Check off key points and LIST them on a separate sheet.
5. ADD and DROP points until you have what you need. Picture your reader and answer this question:

   My reader may be concerned about (what?) so I should mention (what?)

6. Put your points in ORDER. Number them and renumber them until you feel the points follow one another in a logical sequence.
7. Add necessary SPECIFICS (numbers, percentages, dates) and examples.
8. Write any OPENING paragraph that gets to the point. In short, what's the story? What's the bottom line here?
9. Write the middle section, one aspect per paragraph. Draw on your list of points and examples.
10. Write your closing: suggest the NEXT STEP.

Did you notice
   —*it helps to be clear about your purpose before you begin?*
   —*picturing your reader lets you anticipate what the response might be so you know what more to say?*
   —*using a question as a springboard gets you writing?*
   —*it's easier to write once you have something down on paper and can begin to shape it?*

Experiment 31
Send a letter that gets action

Your organization or company needs you to write a letter to get action. What specific things can you do to make people respond favorably to what you say and to take the steps you suggest?

1. Write a letter that gets someone to do something. First decide exactly what you want your reader to do.
   —send a refund?
   —vote against a law?
   —take your suggestions for improving business?
   —speak at your group?
   —correct your bill?
   —buy something?
   —advise you?

2. PICTURE who'll read this letter. Put yourself in her shoes: What would you want, or *not* want, to hear first?

   Write a first sentence that says right out what's the story, but also touches on the interests of or benefits to your reader. Experiment until you strike just the right note. Benefits to the reader might be:
   —getting money or goods
   —creating good will for her company
   —keeping a customer
   —"doing right by" someone
   —being congratulated (sincerely!)
   —being praised (sincerely!)

3. To write the body of the letter and find the most convincing reasons, find the question your letter could answer, put it at the

top of a scratch sheet, and WRITE NONSTOP for five minutes. Sample questions might be:

—How will my reader benefit from what I propose? (If I were in his shoes, what would I want? How can doing what I ask get him that?)

—What good news (praise, money coming) can I put first? (What are the ways this person can improve business?)

4. Underline the best reasons, and "talk out" on paper a few lines about each one. Write up as a paragraph.

—Use *you* more than *I*.

—Omit any parts in which you sound like a crank or a wiseguy: be sure your tone doesn't put people off (check each sentence).

5. Close with a question, or suggest some small action your reader can take right now. Ask for exactly what you want:

—Please credit my account with $214.17 by June 15.

—How can we improve sales? Please send your suggestions by March 10.

6. Read your letter to others, and listen for tone. Ask: what's coming through? Locate and omit any sentences which may get a response you don't want. Keep in mind what exactly you want your reader to do.

7. Type your final draft so the letter looks neat on the page and has no spelling errors.

Did you notice

—if you hedge, or if you tell what the letter's about in the first sentence or as soon as possible?

—you have a new perspective on your letter if you can put yourself in your reader's shoes?

—how important tone of voice is? and how necessary it is to hear what's coming through in what you write?

—any falseness at moments in your letter? or hostility or condescension that you didn't hear but others did?

—if it's useful to write a question with a question mark to encourage a response (as in conversation)? if it's important to spell out one small concrete action the reader can take now?

—a new style or voice emerging that works well for you? what makes for effective communication?

A MODEL LETTER

• Getting someone to change a procedure

MEGATENT RENTALS INCORPORATED
124 Eagle Drive
Newfield, PA 00000
987-123-4567

September 18, 19—

Ms. Georgiana Petrie
Incredible Edibles, Inc.
890 Pleasant View Drive
Newfield, PA 00000

RE: REPORTING COMMISSIONS DUE

Dear Ms. Petrie:

We need your help to eliminate confusion about what commissions are due you. For you to receive your checks promptly, please do the following:

• List commissions due by the billing name (given when the order was placed).
• Send a list of names for the current month only.
• Omit names for which we've already paid you a commission.
• Mail your report by the 24th of each month.

If you have any questions, call me. With your help, we can get things running smoothly. Please send me your next report by September 24. Thank you very much for your cooperation.

Sincerely,

A. L. Licht,
Officer Manger

AL:kt

82

Experiment 32
Persuade with plain English

When you feel there's too much jargon in your writing, and you could be clearer and more to the point, experiment with plain English.

1. Cover up the right-hand column and say aloud in plain English a word or phrase.

WORDS AND PHRASES IN "BUSINESS-ESE"	STAY INSTEAD IN PLAIN ENGLISH[1]
Enclosed please find	Here's, Enclosed is
pursuant to our next meeting	When we next meet
in lieu of	instead of
make inquiry regarding	ask
meets with our approval	we approve
regret to advise	we're sorry
came to my attention	saw
in the event that	if
effectuate, deem, transpire,	_____ , _____ ,
inasmuch as, pertaining to,	_____ , _____

2. Take a phrase or maxim, and "maximize": for fun, put it into business lingo. Use a thesaurus to find long words to substitute for short ones. READ ALOUD to someone: can your listener guess the original?
3. Take a letter, memo, or page from a report, and "make it bad": load it with extra words, legal or business jargon. Write a long, convoluted sentence. Overdo. Use "it is" and "there is" often.

---

[1]Writing in plain English means writing like you speak.

For instance, you've written, "Fear never came into thought." But would you *say* it like that? You'd probably say, "It never occurred to me to be afraid," or, "I wasn't afraid."

Here's your test for plain English: would you say this sentence if you were talking to someone? If not, how *would* you say it?

Read aloud to someone, and notice her reaction. Is your writing so obviously bad, it's funny?

4. Take that letter, memo, or report, and WRITE IT IN PLAIN ENGLISH, trying to be simple, direct, to the point. When you're stuck, and don't know how to say what you mean, try Experiment 50, p. 179.

5. Read aloud your make-it-bad version and your make-it-better version without telling your listener which is which. Is the difference clear? Do some parts sound the same in both? Do you prefer one version? Why?

Did you notice
 —*whether your tone and choice of words suit your meaning? does it sound self-important to use big words when writing about a routine matter?*
 —*whether your plain English version has a helpful "let's work together to get the job done" tone?*
 —*your plain English version is clearer? it's a relief to write that way when giving instructions or explanations?*
 —*the more you try plain English, the easier it comes when you want it? if you're more persuasive and to the point?*
 —*your reader appreciates not having to ferret out your meaning? when you're clear about what you say, the reader is, too?*

TWO VERSIONS OF THE SAME MEMO: WHICH DO YOU PREFER?

BAD MEMO: Too Much Jargon?

Date:

TO: THE CONTROLS TASK FORCE

FROM: Darryl Poole
SUBJECT: Controls

Pursuant to our planned meeting later on this week, we should all review the areas of agreement and findings of the prior meeting held on February 9.

After lengthy discussion we have agreed to some basic needs for definitions as regards RT & Z Controls as referenced during the minutes of the February 9 meeting.

Probably we should reconsider the assignment of control responsibilities as the proper development of guidelines for controls must reside with the most closely associated professional representative of the specific discipline or disciplinary area concerned with delivery and/or administrative responsibility and/or authority. Therefore we should limit our overview level accordingly, and commence by targeting a definition of controls.

GOOD MEMO: Clear Plain English

DATE: February 10, 19—

TO: The Controls Task Force

FROM: Darryl Poole

SUBJECT: Deciding on a Definition of Controls

We left the meeting on February 9 concerned with these questions:

* How much control do we want to develop?
* How do we develop practical control levels without bogging down?
* How can we develop a common vocabulary for systems controls?

Again, how much control do we want to develop? We'll plan to spend much of our next session on this question.

Experiment 33
Liven up your layout

Does the page look uninviting because of large blocks of single-spaced lines that are too dense too read? ADD WHITE SPACE to the page in any or all of these ways.

1. BREAK UP long paragraphs. New idea? New paragraph!

Especially your opening paragraph should be only four or five typed lines. Start a new paragraph when you give a long example or move on to a new point.

2. USE HEADINGS to highlight the main idea.

In reports and long memos, headings can break up the text *and* tell the story. For example, instead of writing "Advantages," give the main idea, like this:

Advantages of Fiber Optics: Faster, Clearer Signals

3. DISPLAY a LIST of selling points, benefits, or key information.

Don't overdo, though. One list on a page is enough! Be sure to display a list only when you want to emphasize the material that is the most important.

Be sure listed items are "parallel," that is, in the same form (and beginning with the same part of speech). The list on the right is parallel and correct:

NOT PARALLEL	PARALLEL: three verbs
Please do the following:	*Please do the following:*

1. *Send a media kit.*	1. ***Send*** *a media kit.*
2. *Success stories of our advertisers.*	2. ***Include*** *success stories of advertisers.*
3. *I'm not sure if last month's sales figures are good enough. Unless they're $25,000 or better, don't mention them.*	3. ***Cite*** *last month's sales figures if they're good enough ($25,000 or better).*

Notice the use of shorter paragraphs, headings, and displayed lists in the following sample report. Also notice that the list is parallel (all nouns).

Did you notice
   —your layout emphasizes what's most important?
   —readers are more eager to read your writing when it looks good on the page?
   —the page looks more inviting when there's enough white space?
   —that headings and lists can draw attention to your key points?

SAMPLE REPORT
USING HEADINGS AND BULLETED LIST

THE EXPANDING MARKET FOR FIBER OPTICS

Electrical contractors want their share of local area networks (LANS) using fiber optics. Contractors who understand the new technology and begin training programs now will lead the field.

Advantages of Fiber Optics: Faster, Clearer Signals

The benefits of fiber optic systems include the following:

• **faster transmission** of data because of the large bandwidth

---

- **lower attenuation** so signals maintain their strength over long distances
- **no interference** by electromagnetic fields (EMI)
- **greater security** because fibers are impossible to tap
- **greater safety** because fibers are insulators so there are never any sparks

In addition, the small size of fibers will increase the capacity of existing conduits by 500%.

Market Factors: Companies Prefer Fiber Optics

By 19––, over half of all corporations in the United States will use fiber optic LANS. The cost of a fiber optic LAN will decrease dramatically, making it the system of choice.

Like most readers, when you pick up a document, you want to know three things: what's it about (main point), what's in it for me (benefits), and what do I have to do (action). *Main point, benefits, action*—that's your formula for writing letters, memos and proposals that get results. You've begun to write this way in Experiment 31 (action-getting letter). The next two experiments will save you time and effort by helping you organize your material instantly.

Experiment 34
Get your request approved: write an "MBA" memo

You need to write an action-getting memo, a request for approval, or a problem-solving memo. Think "MBA":

Main point
Benefits
Action

1. Start with your MAIN POINT. What's needed? What's your request? What's the problem and your proposed solution?

Never mind the slow lead-in or a long paragraph on background. Instead, summarize in three or four sentences what's needed and what you propose.

SUMMARIZE YOUR MAIN POINT

We need to improve the way we present our insurance and pension plans. I propose we purchase 1,000 loose-leaf notebooks at $1.15 each. We can use the notebooks as employee handbooks and simply insert new pages whenever new benefits are negotiated. That way we'll save the cost of printing new handbooks every year.

2. Present BENEFITS to your reader. Put in numbers and percentages to support your point.

BE SPECIFIC ABOUT BENEFITS

Using loose-leaf notebooks will cut costs by 55% and save $2,000 a year.

Benefits can be both tangible (saving dollars) and emotional (feeling good about helping out).

BENEFITS TO READERS

- Save or receive money.
- Save time or effort.
- Solve a problem.
- Get information.
- Get free advertising.
- Make a profit.
- Get things running smoothly.

- Create goodwill.
- Clear up confusion.
- Receive praise, thanks, or congratulations.
- Keep a customer or make a new one.

3. Ask for ACTION by a certain date.

    INSTEAD OF   WRITE

    We look forward to hearing from   *Please send us the information*
    you.   *by March 15. Thank you for*
                                   helping us meet our deadline.

4. Make your SUBJECT LINE specific by putting in an *-ing* VERB (gerund phrase), like this:

    INSTEAD OF   WRITE

    SUBJECT: Filing System   *SUBJECT: Purchasing a New*
                                   Filing System

5. (OPTIONAL) Use an EMBEDDED COMMAND just before your request for action, like this:

    Your approval now will (*help move things along in what way?*)
    OR
    If we (*do what now?*), we can (*benefit how? from what savings in time or money?*)

    Examples:
    Your approval now will help us meet our January 15 deadline. If we purchase the system now, we can have it installed by January 15 at a 20% discount.

6. (OPTIONAL) If appropriate, put in an APPROVAL LINE at the bottom of the page, like this:

If you approve, please sign below and return this page to me by (when?) _____

Place this at the bottom of the page:

Approved by: _____ *Date:* _____

Be sure to picture your reader: will he or she need more information before signing off on your request? You can attach that information. Or, if you feel you're being too pushy asking for a signature at this stage, omit the approval line. Instead, ask for a phone call (give your extension) or suggest times to meet.

Did you notice
   —*the "MBA" formula helps you organize your writing instantly?*
   —*an example can make your point vividly?*
   —*a displayed list emphasizes benefits?*
   —*a request for action makes an effective closing?*

SAMPLE MEMO REQUESTING APPROVAL

Date: February 6, 19--

To: J. M. Dole, Purchasing Department

From: E. M. Smith, Tax Department *EMS*

Subject: Purchasing a Central Filing System

As you know, we've set aside $5,000 in this year's budget to buy a new filing system. I've looked at several alternatives. I think Model 5000 by Document Management Associates (DMA) best suits our needs.

Attached are brochures describing three systems. Below is a quick comparison. Notice that the DMA Model 5000 costs less, holds more folders, and offers all the features of more expensive units.

	DMA 5000	FOX 1000	XYZ #3
COST	$3,400	$4,000	$4,250
CAPACITY (folders)	8,000	6,500	5,000
FIREPROOF	YES	NO	YES
LOCKABLE	YES	YES	YES
INSTALLATION	1 day	1 day	2 days

If you place our order this week, DMA can install the system by February 20. To approve the purchase of DMA Model 5000, please sign below and return this page to me by February 9. Or call me at Ext. 524 if you have questions. Thank you.

Approved by:

Date:

Experiment 35
Bring out benefits in your proposal

Whether you're writing to someone in your company or to a prospective client, offer a plan to fill a need. Organize your proposal the way you did your action-getting memo. Again, think "MBA": Main point, Benefits, Action.

MAIN POINT: What's the the problem and my proposed solution?

BENEFITS: What are the specific benefits to justify the cost?

ACTION: What's the next step for the reader to take?

1. IDENTIFY the reader's needs: state the PROBLEM. Do your research and talk to the people involved. Then clarify the problem by answering these questions:

   WHAT'S THE PROBLEM? WHAT'S NEEDED NOW?

2. Offer a SOLUTION. Briefly, what do you PROPOSE? When and how will you carry out what you propose?

3. Be sure to sound UPBEAT and confident. Avoid the dull lead-in full of generalities. Instead, what can you do for this reader that this reader wants done?

| INSTEAD OF "DULL" | SOUND UPBEAT |

Large complex projects such as refurbishing offices often require a great deal of planning and must take into account many changes due to several variables such as construction and scheduling, purchase plans, stock availability, and fluctuations in corporate staffing.

FURNITURE CONSULTANTS INC. will fully furnish XYZ's new corporate headquarters by May 10, 19––. We will evaluate current inventory, refurbish existing furniture, and dispose of unusable items.

Our services also include tracking on computer all orders, coordinating deliveries, and unpacking items. We will stay within budget and send out written project updates to you each month.

4. Display a list of BENEFITS to the reader that justify the cost. Break out the important advantages or selling points. Let the readers know how much they'll save in dollars or man-hours.

The OV-1000 is a very reliable automatic loader that increases productivity 60–80%. Some of its advantages are as follows:
- *Maintenance takes only ten minutes per eight-hour shift.*
- *Smaller size means more room in the loading area.*
- *Service is always available, 24 hours a day.*
- *Ease of use means less time training personnel.*

NOTE: Make sure the list is parallel: each item should be in the same form (all verbs, or all nouns, or all sentences).

5. Support your statement with SPECIFICS (numbers, names, percentages) to give the proposal an objective tone and to make the benefits concrete. Numbers give credibility to your claims.

   - *50% more durable*
   - *Rated #1 by ABC Inc.*

6. Suggest the NEXT STEP (probably a meeting to discuss plans and cost). Whom should the reader call, at what number?

   We will be pleased to discuss with you materials, costs, and terms. To arrange for a presentation at your convenience, call Arnold Dorrance at 567-1234.

7. (OPTIONAL) Play devil's advocate to TEST your proposal. What will readers raise questions about? What will they object to? How will you respond?

   POSSIBLE OBJECTION:
   MY RESPONSE:

8. Make your LAYOUT look inviting. Aside from a list of benefits, use HEADINGS such as the following:

   Overview: *say what's needed*
   The Problem: *say what it is*
   The Solution: *give it briefly*
   Advantages: *sum up a few*
   The Next Step: *a meeting or a presentation*

Use as your MODEL the sample proposal below.

Did you notice
- —*the "MBA" formula works well in organizing a proposal instantly?*
- —*a displayed list of benefits can be very convincing?*
- —*telling readers the problem even more clearly than they could state it themselves really gets the reader's attention?*
- —*describing a solution right after a problem keeps the reader's attention?*
- —*your layout makes the page inviting when you use headings, lists, and shorter paragraphs?*

SAMPLE PROPOSAL
DONE WITH DESKTOP PUBLISHING SOFTWARE

NEX SYSTEMS, INC.

PROPOSAL
TO INSTALL NEX SYSTEM 2001

Submitted to: William Worth, President, ABC Brothers
Submitted by: Agnes Wells, Vice President, NEX Systems
Date: February 18, 19– –

Overview: The Need for State-of-the-Art Equipment

ABC Brothers requires the highest quality, state-of-the-art telephone equipment in its newly renovated Exford plant. ABC's management recognizes that the current system is slow and inefficient. It does not offer any of the features necessary for the new telemarketing campaign which will begin on May 1.

NEX Systems proposes to fully install Model 2001 by April 15 to enable ABC to achieve the following objectives:

- to have its own **custom-designed system** operating by May 1
- to be ready for a **fiber optic link** between Exford and the company's headquarters in Chicago
- to secure a **lease program** that minimizes cost—with eventual ownership of the system

Advantages: Lower Costs, Increased Efficiency

The NEX System 2001 will cut ABC's current monthly cost from $4500 to $2200 and increase efficiency by at least 75%. Model 2001 is designed to improve productivity and allow for expansion as needed. Its many features include the following:

- state-of-the-art **voice features** such as conference call, call pick-up, automatic call-back, and speed call
- circuit cards for **immediate expansion** of the system as needed
- on-site and remote **programming**
- fully modular units for total system **flexibility**

NEX Systems have been selling and installing telephone equipment for over 20 years. This fall, NEX received the highest rating—in a survey of 500 area presidents of corporations—for superior service and responsiveness to customers' needs.

The Next Step: Meeting to Discuss Costs and Terms

NEX Systems will be pleased to meet with you to discuss equipment, timetable, costs, and terms. To arrange for a presentation in more detail, please call Alex Welch at 000-000-0000, Ext. 123. Thank you for the opportunity of submitting this proposal.

Experiment 36
Display a list of steps in your "how to" memo

Try out the steps yourself while writing down the instructions: that way you'll know exactly what to do when. For a long procedure, write about it in sections (each with a heading) and begin each section with a step #1.

1. DISPLAY A LIST of numbered steps.
2. State ONLY ONE activity PER STEP.
3. Use COMMANDS to begin each step, verbs such as *Do, Use, Create.*

SAMPLE INSTRUCTIONS

How to Sign Out a File

1. *Take the file you need from the cabinet in the file room.*
2. *Write your name and the file name on the Sign-Out Sheet on the desk.*
3. *Return the file to Nancy Drew when you're finished with it.*

Be sure the number itself always stands out with white space around it. If the step continues to the next line, start the second line directly under the text above it, not under the number.

4. Put in EXAMPLES to help the reader grasp the material instantly.

Place examples and explanatory material here, in a separate section BELOW the instruction. Let the step itself stand out with white space around it.

5. Use EVERYDAY WORDS and short sentences.
6. Check to see if the steps are in their proper ORDER. Go through the process yourself, or ask someone to try out your instructions.

7. Anticipate where readers may go wrong and WARN them *before* that step.

For example, write "CAUTION," "WARNING," or "NOTE" if you need to alert readers before they make a mistake, for example:

> *WARNING: BEFORE YOU TURN ON THE COMPUTER, OPEN THE DRIVE DOORS AND BE SURE THERE ARE NO DISKS IN THE DRIVES. They could be erased by mistake.*

Also, if something unexpected may happen (a light flashing, a sound occurring), tell the reader what that event means and what to do then.

> *NOTE: If the **red light** flashes, and the machine does not shut off automatically, push the red RESET button located at the left rear of the unit.*

8. If helpful for your reader, DESIGN A CHART for quick reference.

For instance, for someone learning to use a computer, display information in two columns so the steps are easy to follow, like this:

What Appears on Screen	*What You Do*
1) *Main Menu Display*	*Enter XISO*
2) *"ENTER USERID"*	*Enter your ID code*
3) *"PLEASE ENTER YOUR PASSWORD*	*Enter your password*

Here's another example. Say you need to explain Standard Operating Procedures (SOP). Set up two columns like this:

IF THIS HAPPENS	*DO THIS:*
*A **reporter** calls you for a statement.*	*Refer the caller to Mitch Blaker in Public Relations, Ext. 123.*
*A **customer** complains.*	*Connect the caller with Percy Druid in Customer Service, Ext. 567.*

Did you notice
 —if your list of steps is "parallel" (each step begins with a command)?
 —how a clear layout (a list or chart) can help readers follow instructions?
 —that it's easier to go through a procedure one simple step at a time?

Experiment 37
Summarize so decision-makers know the bottom line

When writing an "executive" summary, try to keep it to one page. What's does the busy decision-maker most need to know? Put key facts up front: deliver your message fast to capture your reader's interest. What's the bottom line here? What's the main point to get across?

1. Read the document you're summarizing. Then, once more, read only the first paragraph, the first sentence of each paragraph, and the last paragraph.
2. WRITE free-flow answering these questions:

    What's the MAIN MESSAGE of this document?

    What are the THREE most IMPORTANT DETAILS to report (main highlights; problem/solution; cost or time involved, benefits)?

3. Write a summary as if you were a newspaper reporter: tell who, what, when, where, why, or how. What's the MAIN IDEA?

    Example: *This report outlines the problems with our current leases and recommends we create a new portfolio.*

4. Put in only pertinent SPECIFICS and important BENEFITS.

Specifics: *The project will take three months and cost $2,500 . . .*

Benefit: *Having people from different regions work on the leases will assure acceptability of the documents in all geographic locations.*

If you can directly quote a person making a key point, do so. Having people speak in your summaries can add interest.

NOTE: If summarizing a magazine or newspaper ARTICLE, be sure to identify (as part of the heading at the top of the page) its author, title, and place and date of publication. Use the third person when speaking about this author's view of the subject: *Shaw outlines four approaches and warns that re-engineering of corporations is useful only if . . .*

5. State clearly the RECOMMENDED ACTION if there is one. Underline it if you like. What's the bottom line? What should our company do with this information? What's the next step?

RECOMMENDATION: *We should use a team to create new state-of-the-art leasing documents.*

Did you notice
—*a new ability to find and express the main points of a document?*
—*that choosing only three details forces you to decide what's most important to get across?*

SAMPLE EXECUTIVE SUMMARY

PROJECT 100:
REVISING OUTDATED LEASES

Executive Summary

Our current leases, developed ten years ago, have become obsolete and impractical. Lately, we've had to use landlords' leases which lead to a less attractive position for tenants and a long period of legal review.

This report outlines the problems with our current leases and recommends we create a new portfolio of documents. The project will take three months and cost $2,500.

The report recommends we use a team to create new state-of-the-art leasing forms. Having people from different regions work on the leases will assure acceptability of the documents in all geographic locations.

The team should consist of three senior regional managers and our real estate counsel. Having our lawyer as a member of the team will ensure legal pre-approval of the language and eliminate the lengthy review of most routine leases.

Experiment 38
Complain in a neutral way

Something's gone wrong. Go ahead and vent your anger in a rough draft—*but throw it away*. Then write a letter in a neutral tone of voice.

Consider that the person receiving your letter—the one who will help straighten things out for you—may not be the one at fault. A plain statement of the facts in an objective tone may be more successful in getting the reader to do what you want.

1. State the PROBLEM: in a neutral and objective way, give an overview of the situation. Take the tone that any fair-minded person reading these facts will want to put things right.
2. Give the FACTS chronologically. What happened first? Then what? Display a list if you like. Give dates.
3. (Optional) REMIND readers why you like their company or why you chose them in the first place (so they'll want to keep you as a customer).
4. ASK FOR *exactly* what you want—a phone call, an apology, a check in a certain amount, a new widget?
5. Suggest a reasonable timetable for response (*within two weeks*).

   Please call me at 000-0000 by March 15 to let me know when you will replace the machine.

6. If appropriate, describe and ENCLOSE photocopies of sales checks, bills, canceled checks, warranties—any material that backs up your claim. Keep copies of everything.

ALTERNATE APPROACH: After a bad experience on an airline, in a bank, or at restaurant, do you want to report what happened *and offer a suggestion* to improve their operation? Take this approach:

1. Praise what you like (or used to like) about them, or state you've been a long-time customer (so they'll want to listen to you).
2. Point out the problem (tell what happened in a neutral tone of voice: put in specifics).
3. Offer a specific suggestion.

INSTEAD OF RANTING	WRITE WITH A NEUTRAL TONE
Do you know how irritating it is to sit hour after hour waiting for a meal? The service at your restaurant stinks.	*On Friday evening, we waited 80 minutes for our entrée.*

Did you notice
—*that controlling the tone makes your letter more businesslike?*
—*that you have more credibility when your tone is controlled?*
—*that asking for what you want specifically will help you get it?*

SAMPLE COMPLAINT LETTER

120 Box St.
Edgebury, CT 06800

February 9, 19--

Mr. John Berman
Director of Customer Relations
Frequent Airlines
1036 East Airport Avenue
Bigtown, PA 00000

Dear Mr. Berman:

I've flown with Frequent Airlines many times, and the service has always been excellent. However, last week I did have a bad experience, and I thought you'd want to know about it. The continuation of my flight was canceled, leaving me stranded for two days. I have not yet received my refund of $210.

On February 4, I boarded Flight 709 from Phoenix to New York with a scheduled stop in Memphis. When we landed there, we waited two hours. We were told the rest of the flight was canceled but we weren't told why.

When I asked for help in booking another flight or arranging for a hotel, the attendant said, "The airline is not required to do that. You're on your own, lady." I couldn't get out the next day, either, because that flight was also canceled at the last minute without explanation. Once again, your staff was neither courteous nor helpful.

Please send me a refund of $210 for the unused portion of my ticket. Also, I'm asking that you reimburse me for the cost of my hotel room ($110). Enclosed is a copy of the bill. I'll look for your check for $330 within the next three weeks. Thank you.

Sincerely,

Belinda B. Buckley
Enc.

Experiment 39
Buffer the bad news

Breaking bad news? Here's the tone to take: it's not that you don't want to do something, but you *can't*—and for good reason.

1. Break the bad news and say you're SORRY.

(Or, if you prefer, explain THE SITUATION first. Put the bad news in context so it's understandable. See Step 2 below.)

We're sorry we can't offer you the funds you requested.

2. Buffer the bad news by putting it in perspective: give SPECIF-ICS (such as numbers).

> *Your credentials are impressive. However, we had over 200 proposals for only 12 grants.*

Numbers can make the reader feel, "You're O.K. You're worth-while. It's just circumstances."

INSTEAD OF	WRITE
We are unable to evaluate your product at this time.	*We're sorry we can't review your product right now. We're completing evaluations of 50 products this month.*

INSTEAD OF GENERALITIES	PUT IN SPECIFICS
Due to the fact that there were a large number of applicants, we cannot offer you the grant.	*This year, we had over five thousand applicants for only two grants, making selection difficult.*

3. Suggest an ALTERNATIVE if possible.

When you can, turn a refusal letter into a letter that conveys useful information.

> *Have you thought of asking the Bigville Corporation of Boston? We suggest you apply to them or any of the organizations we've circled on the enclosed list.*

4. Reassure GOODWILL.

Thank you for your interest in our company. We wish you success with your project.

Did you notice
  —*using numbers, or putting things in context, can take the sting out of bad news so readers don't feel like they're the only ones who failed to get what they want?*

SAMPLE "BAD NEWS" LETTER

JONES MANUFACTURING
502 East Avenue
Ellentown, CA 90001
(213) 876-5432

August 10, 19– –

Ms. Janet Wakowski
18 Royal Place
Bottsville, CA 54398

Dear Ms. Wakowski:

We're sorry we can't offer you the position of administrative assistant. Your credentials are impressive. However, we had over a hundred applicants for only two openings, making selection difficult.

We'll keep your résumé on file and consider you if any other openings occur. We appreciate your interest in our company and wish you success.

Sincerely yours,

Angela Winters
Director of Personnel

Experiment 40
Promote your product, sell your service

You're developing a brochure, sales letter, direct mail piece, or sell sheet. Who is your "target market"? What are their needs, wants, or fears? Keep in mind the "MBA" formula (main point, benefits, action): it can help you organize your material.

1. Decide on your TARGET MARKET. Be as specific as you can about age, sex, job title, location. On a scratch pad, answer this question:

WHO WOULD MOST WANT TO BUY THIS PRODUCT OR SERVICE?

Suburban males in the Northeast with incomes over $50,000? Small business owners in the metro area? Working mothers ages 25 to 50?

2. Search for your SELLING PROPOSITION. What's unique about what you offer?
    a. Ask prospective buyers what they want in this type of product or service. Also, ask them what's out there already, and what's wrong with it. Write down what's said.
    b. On a scratch pad, write free-flow to answer these questions:

    WHAT DO PEOPLE MOST WANT IN THIS TYPE OF PRODUCT OR SERVICE?

    WHAT DO WE UNIQUELY OFFER THAT'S BETTER THAN THE COMPETITION?

3. Write a HEADLINE that speaks to the needs of your target market. Time-tested eye-catching words include these:

    FREE, NEW, INTRODUCING, SPECIAL OFFER, DISCOUNT

Does your headline identify your audience, offer a solution to a problem, or stress benefits right up front? Good! Let readers know quickly why this product is for them.

SAMPLE HEADLINES

FOR VETERANS ONLY: GET A 50% DISCOUNT ON INSURANCE

If you're thinking of relocating, we can help keep costs down.

4. Display a list of BENEFITS. Put in specifics (numbers, dollars saved, percentages), like this:

   THREE GREAT REASONS TO BUY ALL YOUR FILM
   FROM COLOR GALORE, LTD.

   1) *LOWEST PRICES*
      Compare our prices with what you're paying now.

   2) *FREE DEVELOPING*
      With every three rolls of film you buy, we . . .

   3) *HIGHEST QUALITY*
      We offer brand names such as . . . at discount prices.

5. Document your SUCCESS with testimonials and credentials.

What do people say about your product or service? Ask them, and then get their permission to quote them (using names or initial only).

How long have you been in business? Won any awards or received any recognition? How many customers? What's your track record of success?

6. End with an INCENTIVE to act now—and make it easy for the reader to take the next step.

Can you throw in something free as a bonus if the order or inquiry comes in now? Did you put a time limit on the offer to increase the sense of urgency about acting now?

State specifically what to do by when. Call an 800 number? Send in an enclosed business reply card?

   To get your free sample, fill out the enclosed coupon and send
   it to us by March 1, 19– –.

7. Put in PICTURES and design an attractive LAYOUT. Get professional help if you need it.

The "look" of a piece affects whether all your good copy gets read or not! Pictures can tell the story. Good graphic design invites readers to read on. Showing people using the product helps readers put themselves in the picture.

8. Use everyday words and shorter sentences: make every sentence easy to understand.

Did you notice
—the more specific your target market, the more effective your "pitch"?
—that it helps to ask your prospective buyers what exactly they need or want in a product or service like yours?
—an upbeat tone, a clear list of benefits, and a "free" offer can get the reader to take the next step?

SAMPLE PROMOTIONAL PIECE

IMPROVE THE DESIGN
OF YOUR WORKPLACE
SO PEOPLE
WORK BETTER.

Are you planning to move or renovate but are concerned about spending too much money or disrupting operations?

The **Feng Shui Group (FSG)** has helped over fifty Fortune 500 companies improve the workplace and make smooth transitions to new facilities. We will evaluate your workplace, study your plans, and show you how to

---

- **reduce the cost of relocating or renovating by 25-40%**
- **plan for the best use of space**
- **minimize disruption to operations**
- **justify the project's cost to management**

For the **free checklist, "Rate Your Workplace,"** call 1-800-456-9876. Or simply place this brochure in an envelope and return it to us: **FSG, Box 142, Goodchi, CO 12345.**

_____ Yes, send me the free checklist so I can evaluate my workplace.

_____ Please send more information about your service.

Experiment 41
Make news with your press release

Teachers of news writing still use the "inverted pyramid" as the model. Picture a pyramid upside down, with the wide base at the top. Your story is like that: put the most important information first (in case the editor cuts the last paragraphs for lack of space).

1. Look through newspapers at LEADS (first sentences). Clip and collect first paragraphs which tell who, what, where, when.
2. Pretend you're a REPORTER from the local newspaper. You're breaking a story. Write a lead telling who, what, when, where.
3. Tell your story as if it were news (and not merely a thinly veiled puff for your company, product, or organization). What's NEWSWORTHY? What do *you* like to read about?

110

People (What are their accomplishments, background, comments?)

New Products (What's unique or exciting about them? What's new?)

Upcoming Events (What are the details? What's the attraction?)

4. QUOTE PEOPLE. Real voices coming through adds interest to your article.

5. Write consistently in the third person (*XYZ Corporation announces* . . .). Don't use "we" or "you," and don't address the reader. Remember, you're writing as if you were an objective, outside reporter sent *from* a newspaper to write about your company, product, event, or organization.

6. Use shorter sentences and paragraphs. Keep the language SIMPLE. Put verbs in the active voice (tell who did or will do what).

7. (OPTIONAL) End with a blurb about your company or organization. Mention a few positive, pertinent facts to identify it (name, location, product or service, last year's income). You can use this same paragraph at the end of every news release.

ABC Corporation, located in Philadelphia, is a major producer of laser widgets. Its income last year exceeded $90 million.

8. Double space the final draft and use the correct format for a news release.

Did you notice
—*that people speaking in your story adds life and interest?*
—*it helps to pretend you're an objective reporter from outside your organization?*
—*writing like a reporter helps you cultivate a plain, direct style?*

FORMAT FOR A PRESS RELEASE

**LETTERHEAD OF YOUR
COMPANY OR ORGANIZATION**

FOR IMMEDIATE RELEASE
(or give the date you want it released)

For more information, call
(Your Name)
(Your Number)

(OPTIONAL: A HEADLINE HERE IN CAPS)

CITY, STATE, TODAY'S DATE—The lead sentence should spill the beans about who, what, when, where. Continue with your most important fact. Double space the copy. Leave big margins.

Begin a new paragraph when you shift to a new aspect or supply details. Keep your sentences and paragraphs short but not choppy.

Dr. Fran Shaw of the University of Connecticut advises, "Quote people and use quotation marks."

Have you included all the important information people will want to know? To show you've finished, write "END" or ### or

—30—

SHAPING WHAT COMES

Use this checklist to help you sharpen and tighten the drafts of your business documents.

CHECKLIST FOR LETTER WRITERS

- *What response do I want? What would I need to hear to respond like that?*
- *Do I use just the right tone? Talking person-to-person for our mutual benefit?*

Beginning
- *First sentence makes the reader want to continue? Touches on interests or benefits?*
- *Facts up front in plain English? Don't have to wait two paragraphs, or ferret out the meaning?*
- *Good news first? (money coming, what person has been waiting to hear, compliment or thanks when deserved, apology if needed)*

Middle
- *"Here are the facts" step by step?*
- *Specific examples? Best order?*
- *One sentence, one idea? (Too long? Break in two.) One paragraph, one aspect? (Start a new paragraph?)*

End
- *Ask specifically for what you want?*
- *Try a question with question mark?*
- *Suggest some small thing your reader can do now?*

Revising
- *Need to tighten? Cut out extra words. Do I need this sentence at all? Cut out timeworn jargon—sounds better?*
- *Need to sharpen? Too many "it is" and "there was"? Try active verbs instead ("we found," "we sent"). Would you say it like this over coffee? Confusing? Try plain English.*
- *All the facts your reader needs?*
- *Is it clear?*
- *No typos or misspellings? Check a dictionary.*

CHECKLIST FOR MEMO AND REPORT WRITERS

- *Who's reading this, and what does the person want to know?*
- *Concise, complete, clear? In plain English?*
- *Purpose plain? Your tone suits it?*
- *Facts right? No omissions or inaccuracies?*
- *Main points covered? Sequence logical? Paragraphing emphasizes points? Conclusion valid?*
- *Attractive looking? Enough white space? Easy to read? No typos, misspellings?*

Beginning
- *A long report? Start with a summary first: what you found, what it means (what's the bottom line?).*
- *Try out a livelier lead (like the first line of a newspaper story). Key facts first, rather than rambling details?*

Middle
- *Paragraphing and headings stress each of your findings? Most useful order for your reader? Progresses logically?*
- *Define terms, supply examples? Use transitions to smooth the way for easier reading, such as these:*
  For example, First, Second, Next, Thus,

End
- *Ties in with the beginning?*
- *Your "clincher" comes last?*
- *Leaves a clear final impression? Your reader understands what to do?*

AN EXPERIMENT IN WRITING YOUR RÉSUMÉ

"Write a new résumé? But I haven't done anything . . . I don't know what to put on the page . . ." Here's a way to gain confidence and produce a résumé that gets you the interview.

Experiment 42
Redesign your résumé

Part 1: Getting It Down on Paper

1. Write LISTS of details about your BACKGROUND using the questions below as springboards.

> Q1: Where do I work and what do I do there?
> Where did I work and what did I do there?
> Q2: Where and what did I study in school?
> Q3: What am I good at?

2. Write FREE-FLOW glancing at these additional QUESTIONS below to stimulate you while you write. (For Question 1, make notes about each significant job in the past 10 years.)

Q1: *Where did I work and what did I do there?*

What were your responsibilities?
What were you hired to do?
What were your major accomplishments or successes?
What were you praised for?
What did you learn to do?
Did you develop any special skills?
supervise any people?
make any decisions or recommendations?
gather any information?
analyze anything?
report on anything?
get involved in a team effort?
produce any written documents?
help other people in any way?
assume any leadership roles?
How well did you meet deadlines?
Were you ever given any special responsibility for planning, managing, overseeing, supervising?

Q2: *Where and what did I study in school?*

What college-level degrees have you earned or do you expect to earn (by when)?
Can you list any fellowships, scholarships, awards, honors?
Did you ever make the Dean's List?
Did you engage in any special areas of study (pertinent to your chosen field)? What courses?
What about internships or research projects?

Q3: *What am I good at?*

At work, what do people tell you you're good at? (Ask them!)

What have you been praised for?
Do you have any foreign language skills?
What computer skills do you have?
Do you write clearly?
Are you a good problem solver? A good organizer?
What community or volunteer work have you done?

3. Take a few days to EXPAND your LISTS.

Picture what you did *year by year*. Close your eyes and see yourself in that other time and place.

4. Put a CHECK MARK next to items you'll definitely use.

Part 2: Doing a Draft

1. Decide on a FORMAT you like. Look at the sample résumés below or check out books of model résumés at any bookstore.
2. Highlight the skills your future EMPLOYER wants. What job are you after? If you were looking for someone to fill this position, what three qualities or skills would *you* most want? SELECT and rewrite your phrases to bring out those skills most suited to the job you want.
3. EDIT OUT parts that don't support this particular job you're after. (For instance, if you don't want another typing job, don't mention the number of words per minute you type!)

SOME SAMPLE FORMATS AND COMMON HEADINGS FOR SECTIONS

NAME
Home Address
Home Phone

CAREER OBJECTIVE
(State the position or job you want.)

EXPERIENCE
(List and describe most recent job first, and give it the most space.)

EDUCATION
(If you have any post-high school education, list degrees, say what you took where.)

SKILLS AND ABILITIES
(Computer, math, foreign language skills, etc., go here, not hobbies.)

IF YOU'RE SOMEONE WITH LITTLE JOB EXPERIENCE, or in a field (such as teaching) in which educational credentials and degrees are very important, put the "EDUCATION" section first. Give many specifics (courses taken, internships and projects completed) which relate to this particular job you want.

IF YOU'RE SOMEONE WITH A LOT OF JOB EXPERIENCE, try putting a SUMMARY up front of what you offer, perhaps even a bulleted list of your areas of strength, like this:

EXAMPLE OF SUMMARY UP FRONT

SUMMARY: **Technical Support and Service Specialist** with eight years' experience in management and field engineering. Dedicated team leader committed to customer satisfaction and quality service. Promoter of team spirit. Managed national service program. Rated "Significantly Exceeds Expectations" on 95% of all past performance evaluations. Areas of expertise include these:

- *Field Installations, Upgrades, and Relocations*
- *Project Roll-Outs*
- *Nationwide Technical Support*
- *Hardware, Software, and Network Problem-Solving*

Try this format for presenting job history when you want to stress job titles and bring out that you've been given positions of increasing responsibiliity over the years.

SAMPLE FORMAT FOR PRESENTING WORK EXPERIENCE

Position Title Bold and Underlined   Dates of Service

NAME OF COMPANY IN CAPS, city, state abbreviated
Brief description in italics of nature of business and (possibly) revenues.

Describe in short phrases what you did (or do) and your accomplishments. Block these phrases in paragraphs of no more than four or five lines each. Or display a bulleted list, each item beginning with a verb, so the list is parallel.

SEE SAMPLE RÉSUMÉS BELOW, p. 141.

Part 3: Sharpening and Polishing Your Résumé

1. Describe your duties and accomplishments in SHORT PHRASES which begin with DYNAMIC VERBS.

Use the list below of **dynamic verbs** as your springboard: pick your verbs and complete the phrases. What did you do? What results did you get? Use verbs in the past tense for what you've done (*designed*) and present tense for what you do now (*design*).

PICK A VERB AND ADD YOUR SPECIFICS:
Developed *over 50 multimedia presentations for conferences.*
Designed *containers for 35 different products.*
Work with *engineering and marketing departments to determine packaging requirements.*
Trained *and supervised 25 employees.*

LIST OF DYNAMIC VERBS

achieved	controlled	evaluated
adapted	cooperated	expanded
administered	coordinated	explored
advised	created	
analyzed		forecast
approved	dealt with	found
arranged	delegated	
assembled	demonstrated	gained
assessed	designed	generated
attended	determined	guided
	developed	
budgeted	directed	handled
built	distributed	helped
		hired
calculated	edited	
completed	eliminated	identified
conducted	established	implemented
contributed	estimated	improved

increased

inspected

installed

instructed

interpreted

interviewed

issued

launched

lectured

led

maintained

managed

marketed

monitored

negotiated

operated

organized

participated

performed

pinpointed

planned

prepared

presented

prevented

produced

programmed

proposed

provided

recommended

recorded

reduced

reorganized

reported

researched

reviewed

revised

scheduled

set up

simplified

sold

solved

standardized

streamlined

submitted

supervised

supported

taught

tested

trained

translated

used

verified

wrote

won

2. Put in NUMBERS. Specifics give you credibility. State the number of dollars saved, of new customers, of completed brochures. What percentage increase? How large a budget?

INSTEAD OF	WRITE
Administered the budget for the department.	*Administered an annual budget of $1.2 million.*

3. Emphasize PROGRESS, especially if you've been promoted to positions of increased responsibility.

Put your most recent job first and give it the most space. (What gets the most space, gets the most weight.) In any section, put first and say more about items you want to emphasize.

If you're changing fields, what are the portable skills you can highlight which will be important in your new job?

4. Make sure the page looks INVITING and neat. Ask someone to look at it.

- Have you left enough white space between headings and text and paragraphs so they don't seem jammed together?
- Are the headings and names of companies typed consistently in the same way (all capital letters, all boldface, or all underlined)—and do they line up?
- Do important highlights such as job titles stand out clearly?
- Does the page look too skimpy? Or too crowded?
- How can you rearrange, add, or delete material to make the page look neat but full?

5. PROOFREAD—and have SOMEONE ELSE PROOFREAD, TOO. Check spelling in a dictionary. Your résumé MUST be ERRORLESS.

Did you notice
  —a boost in confidence once you've completed your new résumé?

Good work!

SOME MODEL RÉSUMÉS

A SAMPLE RÉSUMÉ BY SOMEONE WITH JOB EXPERIENCE

JANET MOBILITY
431 Center Road
Bentham, NY 00000
(914) 000-0000

FINANCIAL EXECUTIVE

Highly qualified financial executive with ten years' in-depth experience in all phases of accounting in the retail, service, and distribution industries. Demonstrated record of success in effectively evaluating companies' financial condition and implementing programs that meet management's objectives. Key functional strengths include these:

- Accounting Operations
- Financial Reporting/ Analysis
- Cash/Financial Forecasting
- Budget/Control
- Job Costing
- Multistate Payroll
- Administration
- Auditing
- Taxes

EXPERIENCE

Financial Consultant   199- to Present

NEWSTATE SERVICE AND EQUIPMENT, INC.,
  Kerhonkson, NY
Fifteen-million-dollar distributor of truck equipment.

Analyzed financial condition of company. Replaced inadequate accounting system with less expensive PC-based system, increasing operation's effectiveness by

---

50%. Reviewed and contracted new health and liability insurance saving $60,000 annually without reducing benefits.

Created viable business plan for the company. Successfully negotiated extension of line of credit with bank. Reviewed and evaluated several accounting software programs, choosing and installing an appropriate program to meet all departments' needs. Interviewed applicants and hired new Controller. Prepared records for audit by Big 6 accounting firm. Reorganized and updated files. Instituted new policies and procedures in the Operations division resulting in better record-keeping and tighter controls.

Director of Finance   199- to 199-

TURNBULL TRANSPORT LTD., Rochester, NY
Furniture service company serving the Northeast.

Directed day-to-day operations including accounting, administration, and purchasing. Developed and implemented a cash-flow reporting and forecasting system providing president with daily updates. At monthly board meetings, made recommendations to improve profitability. Reduced the reconciliation process of consignment sales from 5 weeks to one week. Supervised an administrative staff of 8.

Controller   199- to 199-

ABC AMUSEMENT TIME, INC., New Paltz, NY
Retail entertainment company with 30 outlets.

Supervised staff of 14 accountants. Promoted to Controller from Accounting Manager after two months.

Processed multistate payroll for 2500 employees. Developed income tax reporting package which reduced Big 6 audit fees by 30%.

EDUCATION

<u>B.S. Degree in Accounting</u>, SUPERIOR POLYTECHNIC INSTITUTE, Franklin, NJ

Grade Point Average of 3.5 out of 4.0. Winner of the Senior Scholar Award. Interned as Project Accountant at Big Hotel Corporation, Los Angeles, CA.

SPECIAL SKILLS

Hands-on experience with Lotus 1-2-3, WordPerfect 5.1, Peachtree and MICA accounting systems, Q & A database software. Speak German. Willing to relocate.

A ONE-PAGE RÉSUMÉ BY A RECENT GRADUATE WITH LITTLE JOB EXPERIENCE

"Education" is placed first and is expanded to include internships and courses which are related to Career Objective. The section also includes awards. Notice how the page is typed for consistency: main headings in caps, job titles and degrees underlined.

MARTIN Q. OXFORD

15 Longwharf Ave.,
Jumpoff, CT 00000
(555) 888-8888

CAREER OBJECTIVE: Mechanical engineer specializing in technical services or process engineering.

EDUCATION:

<u>B.S. in Mechanical Engineering</u>
University of Connecticut
June, 199–

Dean's List. American Society of Mechanical Engineers. Tau Beta Pi. Straight A average in application courses. Have taken several computer and design courses including Advanced Computing, Graphic Design Solutions, Process Engineering in the Nineties, and Drafting. Selected as a Summer Intern (one of ten) to work on the Alaskan Speedline Project. Won the Sturberger Math Achievement Award. Collaborated with professor on design and engineering of the XYZ Project.

WORK EXPERIENCE:

<u>Engineering Assistant</u>
Goddess Construction Co., Johnston, CT
199- to present

Supervise crew of 10 installing heavy manufacturing equipment. Read blueprints. Write weekly progress reports. Assist engineer responsible for troubleshooting. Draft plans. Meet with clients to discuss needs. Praised for attention to detail and problem-solving ability.

SKILLS AND ABILITIES:

Worked my way through college doing construction jobs. Strong analytical and communication skills. Excellent drawing skills. Experienced with all major computer software for engineering design. Fast learner. Willing to relocate.

MODEL APPLICATION LETTERS
TO ACCOMPANY YOUR RÉSUMÉ

Try writing your letter this way:

Paragraph 1: State the job you're interested in and why you're qualified.

Paragraphs 2 and 3: State four or five highlights of what you've done (or are doing now) that are pertinent to this new job you want. If you're responding to an ad, what are the key qualifications asked for? Say how your experience matches those requirements. Sound upbeat.

Paragraph 4: Ask for an interview. Be sure to put in your phone number, and enclose your résumé.

SAMPLE LETTER OF APPLICATION

15 Browne St.
Lakeville, MA 07549

June 16, 199-

Mrs. Janice Soames
Personnel Director
Books-for-Teens, Inc.
111 Wayside Drive
Boston, Mass. 07123

Dear Mrs. Soames:

I'm applying for the job of Writer you advertised in The New York Times. I know I can be useful to you in creating stories and articles for teenagers because my present job is much like that: I write all publicity on a wide range of subjects for the local museum.

My experience fits right in with your requirements. The last three years, I've researched and written over 150 articles on such diverse subjects as spring flowers, pop art, spinning and weaving in the colonies, ice harvesting, staining glass. All these were aimed at the non-technical reader. This year I won the New England Young Writers Award for Excellence. I've published over a hundred articles in regional newspapers, Teen Topics, and Museum Times.

Enclosed is my résumé. I'll be in Boston next week and would like to come by to show you samples of my writing. Would either October 27 or 28 be convenient? Please call me at 617-555-5555. Thank you for considering me for the position.

Sincerely,

Anna Fuerst

Here's another format you can try: a "summary chart." Show how your experiences match the position's requirements.

LETTER OF APPLICATION
BY SOMEONE WITH A LOT OF EXPERIENCE

113 Lewis Street
Bridgeport, CT 08812

April 1, 199-

Mr. James Smith
Vice President, Operations
JDA Software Services, Inc.
50 North Granite Reef Road
Scottsdale, AZ 85250

Dear Mr. Smith:

I am responding to your advertisement for project leaders in News 3X/400 (April 199-). With my qualifications and diverse background in the MIS profession, I know I would be an asset to your organization. For your convenience, here is a list of my qualifications as they line up with your description of the position:

Position Requirements	My Qualifications
Software Design and Implementation	Over 10 years' progressive hands-on experience. Broadbased MIS background with over 7 years' experience in systems design, database design, acquisitions, communications, and programming languages.

Client Contact	Work closely with end-users designing software to meet client's needs. Responsible for ensuring the accuracy of all software systems.
Staff Training	Experienced in recruiting, training, motivating, and developing professional staff and team members.
System Management	Experienced in daily operations and long-term preventive maintenance. Attended IBM technical conference for performance tuning.
Utilities/Languages	Extensive experience working with RPG 111/400, COBOL 400, SDA, PDM, and SEU.

There are additional details on the résumé enclosed. I would be happy to meet with you, and thank you in advance for the opportunity. If you have any questions, please call. My home number is (203) 332-0000.

Sincerely,

Juan Valdez

Chapter 6

Especially for Students Writing Papers

Here are helpful hints nobody may have told you. These experiments will help you feel more confident about what to do when you have to write a paper. You'll generate your own thinking about a subject and end up with a tight paper that makes your point.

HINTS FOR GETTING BY WHAT STOPS YOU

1. Don't be discouraged by the length of the paper or dissertation. Divide the paper into SECTIONS, and start writing the one you can do right now (try Experiment 48). Write the section you're excited about or know the most about. No need to compose the introduction first—you may want to do that last. Just get going wherever you can, and you'll build momentum.
2. Keep an "Ideas" folder for each section. When something occurs to you, write yourself a note and put it in your collection. This material will stimulate you when it's time to write that part.
3. Talk to someone about the place you're stuck, and explain what you have to do. Then write.
4. Work with somebody who's also writing a paper and who concentrates well. Being in the room while someone is writing intently may help you do the same.

HOW TO ORGANIZE A PAPER QUICKLY

You've read, thought, made some notes. Now, what question do you want your paper to answer? Write it like you'd say it. Also, how many pages exactly are asked for? Use that number to help you plan your pages.

Experiment 43
Plan your pages

Before you write, find your focus: do this instant outline.

"PLAN YOUR PAGES" SHEET

TOPIC: _____

NO. OF PAGES ASKED FOR: _____

QUESTIONS MY PAPER WILL ANSWER: (How . . . ? Why . . . ? Does . . . ?)

_____ ?

_____ ?

Page No. of My Paper

p. _____ 1st MAIN POINT: _____
Supporting details or examples: _____

p. _____ 2nd MAIN POINT: _____
Supporting details or examples: _____

p. _____ 3rd MAIN POINT: _____
Supporting details or examples: _____

pp. _____ OTHER POINTS and SUPPORT: _____

p. _____ CONCLUSION: _____

Here are the steps to help you develop a well-organized paper.

1. Read the assignment again. Turn it into one or two specific QUESTIONS your paper could answer. Brainstorm several possible questions. Write them in simple language using everyday words.

HOW _____ ?
WHAT _____ ?
WHY _____ ?
OTHER QUESTIONS _____ ?

(OPTIONAL) Show your list of possible questions to your teacher to help you select the ones you'll explore in this paper.

QUESTION(S) MY PAPER WILL EXPLORE:

_____

You'll place these questions at the end of your first paragraph. However, if your teacher has asked specifically for a **thesis statement** in paragraph 1, do this next step.

2. Turn your question into a THESIS statement.
   a. Write free-flow using your questions as a springboard. You need to write some of your paper to discover your thesis.
   b. Turn your question into a sentence which answers that question and provides the "controlling idea" you'll prove in the paper.

TIP: As your paper moves from rough to first draft, revise your thesis so it *fits* the paper that's evolving.

THESIS MY PAPER WILL PROVE:

_____

You'll place your thesis statement at the end of paragraph 1.

3. Identify KEY WORDS you'll want to "thread" through your paper.

You'll use these words a few times throughout the paper to keep your own and your reader's mind close to the point. Take your key words from the assignment as given, from your questions, from your thesis, or from the title of your paper. What is your paper really about?

KEY WORDS: _____

_____

_____

4. After filling in your "Plan Your Pages" Sheet, look at it often as you write your ROUGH DRAFT so you don't stray from your focus.

For example, if you planned to be on page two when you got to the second main point, are you? Or have you gone off on a tangent and are writing too many pages you'll have to cut? Here are some more tips to help you write:

OPENING PARAGRAPH: End with your questions or thesis.

FIRST MAIN POINT becomes Paragraph 2 of your paper. Does your first point follow from the questions or thesis you posed in Paragraph 1? What is your reader expecting to read here?

SUPPORTING DETAILS AND EXAMPLES: What passages from books can you quote or what examples can you give to support your first main point?

SECOND MAIN POINT: Include a KEY WORD from your title, questions, or thesis, so we know you're staying on point. Use transitions such as: *In addition, In contrast, First, Second.*

CONCLUSION: Save your "clincher" for last. Does your ending tie in with opening questions or thesis? Can you use *Thus* or *In conclusion* to signal you're concluding?

Did you notice
   —*how a few minutes of planning at the beginning can get you going, build confidence, make writing the paper less random?*

—*your planning sheet saves time so you don't "go off on a tangent" and write a lot of pages you'll later discard as beside the point?*

—*you have a better sense of the paper as a whole even before you begin?*

—*you stay focused more easily?*

EXAMPLES OF QUESTIONS, THESIS, KEY WORDS

ASSIGNMENT: Discuss the six ancient civilizations in terms of how successful they were.

SAMPLE SPECIFIC QUESTIONS TO END PARAGRAPH 1

What is the measure of a "successful" civilization? Which of the six ancient civilizations (Mesopotamia, Egypt, Palestine, Persia, Greece, and Rome) was most successful in providing its citizens with both personal satisfaction and a secure defense?

SAMPLE THESIS STATEMENT

Of the six ancient civilizations (Mesopotamia, Egypt, Palestine, Persia, Greece, and Rome) only two offered their citizens both personal satisfaction and a secure defense. By these criteria, then, Egypt and Rome were the most "successful" of the ancient civilizations.

Do you see how both passages "frame" everything to come? Your reader expects that the next paragraphs will take up, in the order given, six different civilizations and whether they offer (here are your *key words*) personal satisfaction and secure defense.

SAMPLE TOPIC SENTENCE FOR PARAGRAPH 2

One of the oldest recorded civilizations, Mesopotamia increased the personal satisfaction of its people by establishing a farming com-

munity. People no longer had to wander for long periods in search of food.

SAMPLE TOPIC SENTENCE FOR PARAGRAPH 3

Egypt surpassed Mesopotamian civilizations by offering both a high degree of personal satisfaction and a secure defense.

SAMPLE TOPIC SENTENCE
WITH A TRANSITIONAL PHRASE

Unlike Mesopotamia, Egypt offered a secure defense for its people as well as a much higher degree of personal satisfaction.

When you plan your pages, you don't spend a lot of time gathering and writing an unwieldly amount of material you won't use.

Example: Your Plan for a Five-Page Paper

p. 1 First paragraph—Introduction
Perhaps open with A PROVOCATIVE QUOTATION that's a takeoff point. Use one from the reading you've done.

ASK THE QUESTION (with a question mark) that this paper will answer.

Second paragraph, further paragraphs
Do you need to DEFINE TERMS? Give any more background? Do it here or else go on to the **FIRST ASPECT** that needs to be discussed.

You may need more than one paragraph, but keep to ONE PARAGRAPH, ONE ASPECT.

Support main statements with a quotation from one of your sources. MAKE YOUR CASE.

p. 2 **SECOND ASPECT** (with examples)

p. 3 **THIRD ASPECT**   (")

p. 4 **FOURTH ASPECT** (")

p. 5 Last paragraph—Conclusion
Reread your first paragraph. ANSWER the question: so, what's the bottom line on all this?

As you write the paper, check your plan. If you see you're already on page 3 and you've only given background material, you know it's time to answer the question (or reword it!). If you don't have enough pages to go into all the aspects, you could touch on most of them briefly, then say, "but the main one is . . . ," and write the paper largely on that one.

Go into more detail, or include more aspects, if the paper is to be ten pages. But PLAN YOUR PAGES in any case, and check your plan as you write. It'll keep you from going off the track or writing forty pages and then trying to pare them down to four.

TRY THIS TO ORGANIZE A PAPER

Introduction—*Opening quotation.*
Question you'll answer.
Define terms?
Body—*First aspect.*
Second aspect (new paragraph).
Third aspect (new paragraph . . . or more).
Conclusion—*Sum up, tie in to opening.*
Answer your question.

WRITING A SCIENTIFIC, TECHNICAL, OR LAB REPORT

███████

Experiment 44
Use "There is" instead of "I think"

You've read the literature, run your experiments, and you're ready to tell what you've found. NOTE: If your teacher provides a format, be sure to follow it.

1. DIVIDE your report INTO SECTIONS. MAKE UP A QUESTION you could answer for each section, such as:

Title *Abstract*[1]	WHAT DID I FIND, AND WHAT DOES IT MEAN? (Briefly, your major findings with just enough explanation of what was done so they have meaning)
Introduction→	WHAT'S BEEN DONE OR SHOWN ABOUT THIS ALREADY? (Surveying the literature, defining a principle, or giving your hypothesis)
Materials → *and Methods*	WHAT DID I USE IN MY EXPERIMENT, AND WHAT DID I DO FIRST, SECOND, NEXT?
Results →	WHAT HAPPENED? (or) WHAT'S THE STORY ABOUT THIS PHENOMENON? (Just the facts; what do your graphs and tables show?)
Discussion →	WHAT DO THE RESULTS MEAN? (Interpret your findings in light of other research)

---

[1]To write an abstract, see p. 140.

Conclusion →   WHAT HAVE I SHOWN? IMPLICATIONS OR FUTURE DIRECTIONS?
(Your conclusions?)

2. Choose the question you feel you can write about now, and freely talk out the answer on paper.
3. Try doing another section the same way. Take a break when you need it: walk around, stretch, have an apple, relax face and limbs. Then try the question, writing nonstop.
4. Write your first draft, in logical order, beginning to end.

To take on the scientific or impersonal tone of voice appropriate to this kind of report, SUBSTITUTE "there is," "one sees," and "we find" wherever you write "I think."

Or take "I" out by turning the sentence around like this:

Instead of	*Write*
•I put the rats on a schedule of	→The rats were placed on
•I cut the crystal into	→The crystal was cut

OR: substitute "one" for "I"

•I think that	→One sees that
•It is my opinion that	→There is

5. If describing a PROCESS, check to see whether you've told the whole story, not omitting any important step. Move through each stage, show its function and its relationship to the whole. Have you found a clear illustration everyone can understand to explain the PRINCIPLE involved here?
6. TRY OUT your first draft on someone outside your field. Ask her to stop you whenever she hears something confusing: where does she get lost?

Did you notice
    —if you've made something clearer to yourself and your reader?
    —if your facts arrive one by one?
    —if a reader can follow (and duplicate) what you've done?
    —where you need to use plain English to explain something more clearly?

WRITING AN ABSTRACT

Your report requires an abstract of 200 words. Use the approach in Experiment 48 to get words on paper.

Head a sheet of paper with each of the questions below, and WRITE NONSTOP, "talking" on paper:

   I. WHAT WAS DONE?

  II. HOW WAS IT DONE?

 III. WHAT WAS FOUND?

Use the impersonal tone when you do your first draft. Construct sentences to avoid using *I*. Present your findings as facts: an objective account that sums up what you discovered.

1. Make sure your abstract can stand alone.

   Don't write *"See page 10"*—that is, don't refer to page numbers or sections in the document.

2. Keep the language simple.
3. Reflect the most important contents of the document.
4. Take a neutral tone: sound objective about the material.

A SAMPLE ABSTRACT

ABSTRACT OF

"The Growth of Laser Widgets in the U.S. from 19– to 19–"
by R. J. Williams

Twenty major users of five brands of laser widgets were surveyed in 19– and 19–. Data was collected about price, durability, delivery time, distribution channels, and sales projections. This study analyzes the benefits and drawbacks of each of the five major laser widgets on the market.

> Williams describes the widespread acceptance of all brands in the U.S. over the past two years. The study projects the continued growth of laser widgets at a rate of 7% a year through 19–.

WRITING ABOUT LITERATURE

Experiment 45
Immerse yourself, discover your slant

---

1. CHOOSE a writer or work you really enjoy and want to spend time with.
2. READ as much as possible, especially when you want fresh food for thought. Immerse yourself in this writer's novels, stories, poems.
3. COLLECT IN YOUR NOTEBOOK striking passages or quotations. If lengthy, write the opening line, and a note about the rest. Be sure to write down book and page number. Look for
   —recurring *themes* or ideas, and changes in themes
   —repeated *images* and *words* (*live, wake, wind, birch*)
   —*striking lines* (vivid, well-said, moving)
   —favorite *stylistic devices* and *variations in techniques* (from earlier to later works)
   (Does this author ask rhetorical questions? Coin words? Use slant rhymes? Very length of sentences? Use sensory specifics or abstract terms?)
4. READ LETTERS and essays about writing, by your writer.
   How does this person see the creative process? the aim of a writer? Write down striking quotations, book, and page number.
5. Start a "THEY SAY" folder or section in your notebook. Look up your writer in the card catalogue at the library, and find out what others say about her work. Or search through critical

editions and anthologies of essays about her (bookstores carry these). Jot down any statement that strikes you, and note author, title, city of publication, year, and page number.

6. DISCOVER YOUR SLANT. First, read through your notes and underline highlights. Set aside. Write across the top of a blank sheet: "What strikes me about this author's writing?"

7. Pick up the sheet, and write nonstop by "talking out" whatever occurs to you. Keep the pen moving. Begin anew with any sentence. Cover two pages if you can.

8. Read over, underline highlights, and see if you can ASK YOURSELF THE QUESTION YOU WANT TO ANSWER about this person's work. Place that quotation on the top of another sheet. Ask something such as

—What's the best part of this writer's work?
—How are her early writings like (or unlike) her later ones?
—What themes recur? What images?
—What techniques of style stand out?

9. WRITE QUICKLY by "talking out" the answer. Go!

Did you notice
  —*what attracted you to this writer? has that changed?*
  —*if reading what others say about her helped you appreciate the writer's work, or made you feel you missed something? did it make you want to read more or not?*
  —*if you became interested in your writer's life, and how it fed her work?*
  —*if you share the writer's view of the world?*

SHAPING WHAT COMES

BEGINNINGS

You know what aspect of a writer's work you'll explore, and you've discovered your slant. You want to show a progression in ideas or techniques from earlier to later works. Or you want to trace one theme. Whatever your focus, let your reader know right away what your paper's about.

To open: Find a provocative or representative quotation, from the writer's work or from a critic's commentary, which serves as a good takeoff point. From there, you can elaborate, illustrate, agree, or disagree.

Or, try this: ask your reader the question you're going to answer in this paper. A question helps your reader to focus, and makes her want to read on.

As you write your opening and the paper, you might want to follow the conventions for writing about literature. For example:

1. Write "we find" and "one sees" instead of "I think" and "my impression is." Use the impersonal tone of voice.
2. When quoting the writer's work or a critic's comments as they appear in print, USE THE PRESENT TENSE (*McKay calls Thoreau "the philosopher of environment"*).

Some Sample Openings

"The Lottery" tells the story of good neighbors in a small town who annually stone to death one of their own in hopes of a good harvest. Using symbolism and understatement, Shirley Jackson paints a disturbing picture of people as automatons acting out of habit, superstition, and fear.

* * *

Nowhere do we find such a complete summary of Walt Whitman's thought than in "Democratic Vistas." According to Whitman, what are the needs and what is the promise of this grand experiment America?

* * *

One can approach Emerson's essays "The American Scholar" and "Montaigne: or, The Skeptic" as earlier and later versions of his thought about mankind. What has happened to man that he must be either parrot or skeptic? And what is the remedy?

* * *

MIDDLES

What you say in your opening paragraph should lead naturally into the rest of your paper. If you're not sure how to organize your material, try one of the patterns suggested below.

Plan A: Technique Discovers Theme

Looks over your material, and underline or put checkmarks next to striking examples of this writer's techniques and themes.

When you consider the themes, what main ideas emerge and recur? Some view of man and his condition? A statement about how we live? List prominent themes; note important passages.

What about techniques? Look closely at the way this writer uses words, phrases, and sentences. How does she build momentum, begin and end sentences? Do you notice that certain words or images are repeated? Does she use jargon, formal words, slang, or plain English? To what effect? Does the writer use mostly sensory specifics or abstract language? Short sentences or long? Tie in *how* he says things with *what* he says.

For example, you're writing about Emerson's exploration of "what man can know." You might expect the author to pose abstract questions like a philosopher. But you find a striking passage in "The American Scholar" which uses concrete sensory specifics, and you point out Emerson's choice of words:

> What would we really know the meaning of?
> The meal in the firkin; the milk in the pan;
> the ballet in the street; the news of the boat;
> the glance of the eyes, the form and gait of
> the body. . . .[1]

---

[2] Ralph Waldo Emerson, "The American Scholar." *Selections from Ralph Waldo Emerson's*, ed. Stephen E. Whicher (Cambridge, Mass., 1957), p. 78.

144

Emerson brings the question back to one's experience here, in this body now in this place. His meaning is mirrored in his choice of words, these sensory specific examples.

Plan B: They Say/I Say

"Statement of the question, negative solution, positive solution"—a strong way to make your case.

In the opening paragraph, ask the question your paper will answer. Be sure to end with a question mark.

In the next paragraph(s), give what others have said about this question, as a background and framework for what you'll say later. What issues about this writer and her techniques does this question raise? Be sure to footnote any direct or reworded passages from critics.

Write a brief transition, a bridge from what "they say" to what "I say"—but don't use *I.* You're going to tell what you think about all this, but use the impersonal "one sees" and "we find."

For the main part of your paper, give your slant, point by point, so the reader gets a sense of something building. Support with quotations from your writer's work (your "primary" source).

We see that Thoreau . . .

One notes the way in which Whitman . . .

Faulker himself describes the way he writes in . . .

The speaker[3] of the poem begins by naming . . .

Plan C: Chart Out Your Comparison/Contrast

Decide what you'll compare or contrast.

You've planned to show similarities and differences in a writer's earlier and later works. So you've chosen three characteristics of her poetry that will help you make a point about a change in the quality of her perception and expression. You'll discuss these items:

---

[3] It's conventional to refer to "the speaker" of a poem rather than giving the poet's name, so you preserve the distinction between the poet and the voice she's chosen to use in this one particular poem.

(1) recurrent images
(2) use of rhyme
(3) meter

For a balanced presentation of your material, see Experiment 46, pp. 149–152.

ENDINGS

Read your beginning so you write an ending that ties in. Let your reader know that you're concluding: "Thus, we see that . . ." Try any of these ways to end:

1. ASK YOUR QUESTION (in slightly different words?), and give a succinct answer.
2. Sum up your main points.
3. Offer a clincher (one final piece of evidence).

For a thought-provoking final sentence,

4. Use one last quotation from your writer that seems to sum it all up for you.
5. Briefly suggest a further line of exploration, the next question.
6. Briefly point out the wider significance of your ideas.

Have you left your reader with a strong single impression?

TITLES

This is a good time to look at the title for your paper. Does it say what your paper's really about?

Your title should be specific. Try to include the name of the author, the work, and the aspect you'll discuss, like these:

SAMPLE TITLES FOR PAPERS ON LITERATURE

Setting and Theme in Crane's "The Open Boat"

Ironic Elements in Updike's "A & P"

Wordsworth's Lyrics: The Poetry of Wise Passiveness

SETTING UP QUOTATIONS

When you quote a few lines, use quotation marks around the exact words of someone else, like this:

The story takes place on a clear, sunny day with flowers "blooming profusely and the grass . . . richly green" (74).

Note that the quotation marks begin around the exact words from the text. The ellipses (three dots) are used to indicate that some words from the original text are missing in this excerpt. The number in parentheses before the period refers to the page number where this quotation appears in the original text. (See "Citing Sources" below.)

When you quote three or more lines, block the whole passage five spaces in from the margins and omit the quotation marks, like this:

The community and even the children in the story participate in the stoning of the "winner" of the lottery.

> *Bobby Martin had already stuffed his pockets full of stones, and the other boys soon followed his example, selecting the smoothest and roundest stones (74).*

CITING SOURCES:
USING IN-TEXT NOTES INSTEAD OF FOOTNOTES

When you include ideas and quotations from other people, books, and journals, you must identify your sources.

Instead of using footnotes, the Modern Language Association (MLA) recommends using *in-text notes* which refer to a list of Works Cited at the end of paper. A *signal phrase* within your sentence identifies the **author**, and all you need do is put the page **number** from the source in parenthesis, like this:

According to **Matthiessen**, Wordsworth suffered "a great falling off in genius" in his later years **(225)**.

If you don't use a signal phrase, use the author's last **name** and the page **number** in parentheses, like this:

Whitman "is America . . . his time and his people" **(Pound, 8)**.

If your Works Cited page has more than one book by that same author, use an abbreviated version of the book's title instead, like this:

Whitman "is America . . . his time and his people" **(Poets, 8)**.

Your Works Cited page gives a full bibliographical citation of every reference you consulted, all listed alphabetically. For a sample list, see Glossary, p. 191. Here is the basic model:

Works Cited

Last Name of Author, First Name. *Title of Book*. City of publication: Name of Publisher, year of publication.

Shakespeare, William. *The Tragedy of Macbeth*. New York: Washington Square, 1959.

For a concise summary of how to do in-text notes and Works Cited, see Diana Hacker's *A Writer's Reference*. Or consult the *MLA Handbook for Writers of Research Papers* (Modern Language Association of America, 10 Astor Place, New York, NY 10003).

A paper for English class would certainly follow the MLA style. However, your psychology professor may prefer conventional footnotes or the APA style (American Psychological Association).

WRITING ABOUT PEOPLE, ERAS, OR IDEAS

This experiment will help you write a comparison/contrast.

███████

Experiment 46
Choose three bases of comparison

This approach will help you economize your time.

1. Decide what two people, eras, movements, or philosophies you'll compare or contrast. X and Y.
2. WRITE QUESTIONS you could explore
   —HOW IS X LIKE Y?
   —HOW WAS X UNLIKE Y?
   —WHAT'S WORTH FINDING OUT ABOUT X AND Y?

3. Narrow your subject as much as you can. For instance, MAKE A LIST OF ITEMS (qualities or characteristics) you might explore.
   Here's a sample:
   You want to discuss the *Book of Job* and also *Ecclesiastes*.
   You could look at each one's:
      structure   ←YOUR
      themes   LIST
         (man's relationship to God,
         man's relationship to man)
      impact
      way of concluding

4. Choose three items as your "bases" of comparison or contrast. Choose the points that interest you most. (You can discuss other items as well if you're asked to write a longer paper.)
5. Before writing, PLAN YOUR PAGES. Get an overview of what

149

you need to do, according to how many pages you've been asked to write. Here's a sample plan:

> Length of paper: 8 pages plus bibliography
> Beginning: ½ page
> Middle: about 6 pages
> End: 1 page

Then ask yourself: In six pages (the body of the paper), how many items of comparison/contrast could I cover well?

For example, compare X and Y in terms of items 1, 2, 3

> Figure: 1 page on each item, about X, equals 3 pages.
> 1 page on each item, about Y, equals 3 pages.
> Total for Middle: 6 pages

If you know in advance you have only about six pages for the body of your paper, and exactly what you'll write about on each (for a balanced comparison), you'll know what kind of and how much material to get from books.

But be open: perhaps after you research your subject, you may want to discuss only one item in depth.

6. Find the books that seem most helpful, and look up key words (X, Y, the items) in the index. Read the appropriate pages, make notes, jot down striking quotations, plus author, book title, city of publication, year, and page number.
7. To begin writing the paper, ASK YOURSELF a question about each item. WRITE it across the top of a sheet, and then answer it by writing nonstop:

Are X and Y basically similar or different in _____ (your item 1)?

8. Write your thesis. Mention all three items, and the overall similarity or difference between the two main things (X and Y) which you'll discuss. If you're stressing similarity, phrase it opener like this:

YOU → Although the *Book of Job* and *Ecclesiastes* differ in
WRITE structure, they share certain themes, and end in the
say way.

If you're stressing differences, you might write:

YOU→   The *Book of Job* and *Ecclesiastes* have certain themes in
WRITE   common; however, they differ greatly in structure and
in the way they end.

9. Put together a first draft: use your thesis (step 11) and your
discussions of each item. Supplement with quotations to
support what you say.

Begin a new paragraph for each idea you discuss.

SHAPING WHAT COMES

For a balanced comparison, you want to stick to just those
bases of comparison (items 1, 2, 3) you chose, and give
equal space to each.

Here are the two plans for arranging a comparison or
contrast of X and Y. Either you write about X first, discussing
each item in a separate paragraph, and then do the same for
Y. Or you might take item 1, write one paragraph about X,
one about Y, and go on to item 2 and 3 in the same way. Like
this:

X—the idea, person, era, book you're comparing to
Y—the other idea, person, era, book
1, 2, 3—your three (or more) bases of comparison (items to
be discussed about X and Y)

Organize horizontally:→
1st paragraph: X 1   then 2nd paragraph: Y 1
3rd paragraph: X 2   then 4th paragraph: Y 2
5th paragraph: X 3   then 6th paragraph: Y 3

Or, organize vertically↓
1st paragraph: X 1
2nd paragraph: X 2

3rd paragraph: X 3
>> Transition ("In contrast" or "Similarly")
>> 4th paragraph: Y 1
>> 5th paragraph: Y 2
>> 6th paragraph: Y 3

Of course, it may take more than a paragraph to discuss item 1 about X ("Julius Caesar's goals"); just be sure to give equal time to item 1 about Y ("Mark Antony's goals").

CHECKLIST FOR PAPER WRITERS

—*Does the opening sentence give my subject and my slant, and lead into the items discussed next?*
—*Do I support my statements with specifics, such as quoted material? Two examples at least for each point I make?*
—*Do I stick to "one paragraph, one aspect," and not go off on a tangent? Any sentences that don't belong or should be moved?*
—*Do I stick to the base of comparison I chose, giving "equal time" to each side of the comparison/contrast?*
—*Do I use enough "TRANSITIONS" to begin paragraphs and prepare my reader for a shift in ideas?*

ABOUT TRANSITIONS

Here are some useful words to begin paragraphs and signal what you're doing.

What you're COMPARING what just came with what's coming:	When you're CONTRASTING what just came with what's coming:
Too,	In contrast,
Similarly,	However,
Likewise,	Unlike,
In the same way,	On the other hand,
. . . share . . .	. . . differ . . .
. . . have in common . . .	. . . do not share . . .

When you're CONCLUDING,
typing in what just came
with your final words:

Thus,
Therefore,
So we see,
In conclusion,
To sum up,
Finally. . . .

See page 174 for a list of more transitions you can use.

WRITING ABOUT PUBLISHED ESSAYS

You've been asked to read an article or published essay and to discuss it. Here's a way to help you review both content and presentation.

Experiment 47
Critique an article's effectiveness

1. BEGIN your review with a startling fact or statistic related to the topic at hand, or choose a provocative or controversial quote from the article or essay you've just read.

Your opening will attract readers' interest and bring them immediately into the world of the essay, the topic under discussion.

2. End your OPENING PARAGRAPH with the QUESTIONS you'll answer about this article, or with a thesis statement you'll support.

Say what this article aims to do or comment on how successfully it accomplishes its aim. In what way is this writer's view interesting? Is the view presented effectively?

SAMPLE QUESTION TO END FIRST PARAGRAPH
How valid is Bird's comparison of a liberal arts education to a religion?

(or)

SAMPLE THESIS STATEMENT
TO END FIRST PARAGRAPH
However, Bird's comparison of a liberal arts education to a religion lacks convincing examples and uses too many quotations.

3. Outline the author's MAIN IDEAS.
4. Give your CRITIQUE and SUPPORT it with quoted passages.

REVIEWING FOR CONTENT (IDEAS): Offer contrary or additional viewpoints you've found in other authors or state your own views. Do you agree or disagree? With some of it or all of it?

REVIEWING FOR PRESENTATION (ORGANIZATION AND STYLE):
   a. Point out important SHORTCOMINGS that get in the way of the article's effectiveness. Are there any of the following: omissions, hard-to-follow organization, hard-to-read sentences, lack of supporting examples, flaws in logic, argumentative or sarcastic tones? Quote specific places that are flawed, and point out, for each one, how it undermines the essay.

(or)

   b. Give the STRENGTHS of the article. What's convincing about its ideas and the way they're presented? QUOTE the most convincing and well-expressed sentences.

5. CONCLUDE by answering any of these questions:

How does this article change our view of the topic? How effective is this article in convincing the reader? How should we think about this topic now? What, if anything, should we *do*?

Did you notice
   —*how the writer's style can make the article more or less persuasive?*

—*the ways in which a writer convinces a reader by appealing to both reason and emotion?*
—*that vivid examples, telling statistics, and apt quotations are effective ways to involve and persuade the reader?*

PEER REVIEW:
COMMENTING ON ANOTHER STUDENT'S PAPER

Be positive, gentle, and specific when commenting on another student's paper. Follow the "COST" Formula to do a peer review. Consider the paper from the point of view of its

Content
Organization
Style
Technical Errors

Here are the steps, followed by the PEER REVIEW SHEET for you to fill in.

1. Read the essay, then write free-flow your MAIN IMPRESSIONS of what the writer does well and what the essay most needs now.
2. Check for adequate CONTENT.

If the draft is at such an early state that there is not enough content or focus, don't go on to the next steps. Instead, help the writer find a specific focus by doing Experiment 43, "Plan Your Pages." Or suggest a more specific thesis statement (or controlling questions) for paragraph 1.

3. Check for logical ORGANIZATION, so the essay stays focused and builds its case.
4. Point to places where the writer can improve STYLE by revising sentences which need to be better expressed.

THEN, FOR "ALMOST FINAL" DRAFTS ONLY . . .

5. Proofread for TECHNICAL errors (grammar, punctuation, spelling).

HINT: Break for a few minutes before proofreading so you can take a fresh look.

PEER REVIEW SHEET

WHAT DO YOU LIKE ABOUT THIS ESSAY? _____

WHAT DOES THIS ESSAY MOST NEED NOW? _____

WHAT'S THE MAIN IDEA BEING PROVEN OR EXPLORED? _____

Content

Yes No
❑ ❑ Can you identify the thesis statement or controlling question?
    Mark it with an X in the margin.
❑ ❑ Is it specific enough?
❑ ❑ Is there sufficient content yet for an essay?

IMPROVED THESIS OR CONTROLLING QUESTIONS: ___

Organization

Yes No
❑ ❑ Does paragraph 1 "frame" for the reader what's to come?

❑ ❑ Does paragraph 2 "follow" from paragraph 1 (begin to answer the question, support the thesis, or define terms)?
❑ ❑ Does the ending tie in with the beginning?

IMPROVED CONCLUSION: _____

In the margin, POINT OUT SENTENCES which need

❑ To begin with a **transition** (*In contrast, However, Unlike, Moreover*)

❑ To remind us of the focus by repeating a **key word** (from the thesis, controlling question, or title)
❑ To be supported by an **example**, statistic, or quotation to prove the point
❑ To be **moved** (would work better elsewhere)
❑ To be **cut** (repetitive, unnecessary)

Style

Place a question mark in the margin NEXT TO SENTENCES which

❑ Are awkwardly expressed or confusing
❑ Have the wrong tone (too harsh), or sound too informal (slang?) or too formal (jargon?)
❑ Begin with the vague *This*?
   (Can you suggest a noun to put after the word *This*?)
   This _____

A MORE SPECIFIC OR BETTER TITLE FOR THIS PAPER WOULD BE:

For your proofreader's checklist, see p. 181.

FINDING YOUR WAY FROM NOTES TO FIRST DRAFT

There are many ways to get moving so you can immediately write whatever you want.

If you have *no idea* what to write about, see "How to Find What You Want to Write" (below).

If you have a *subject*, and want to narrow it, and start writing, see "Suppose I Have a Subject—Now What?" (p. 160).

If you already have a specific *question* you want to answer, turn to Experiment 48, page 161.

HOW TO FIND WHAT YOU WANT TO WRITE

WRITE across the top of a page: "What would I like to write about?" Do your relaxation exercise (p. 13). "TALK on paper"[1] nonstop for a page. Do this again at another time. Underline highlights: Do you see anything worth developing?

Or, let your environment and your own writing stimu-

---

[1] Rudolph Flesch and others use the phrase "talk on paper" to mean write as you speak, in plain English. I mean it to imply that you can write as easily as you talk. To "talk on paper," here, means free-flow nonstop.

late you. Follow through on an item or two from the lists below. Write nonstop for five minutes.

WHERE TO LOOK	*WHAT TO TRY*
your "Ideas" folder (see p. 6)	eavesdrop
diary	observe people in pressure situations
journal	observe people in social situations
dreams you wrote down	interview people
newspaper headlines	record a conversation
your "Clippings" folder (see p. 6)	record a fight
advice-to-lovelorn column	imagine the best thing that could happen now
parties	pretend you're a . . .
hobbies	imagine a modern hero
gravestones	redo a dream's ending
family photos	watch the wind in the trees
myths	imagine. What if . . . ?
the Bible	talk about what's worth knowing
history books	make up a writing experiment
maps	go somewhere new, and notice!
paintings	
your ethnic background	
the landscape	

"SUPPOSE I HAVE A SUBJECT—NOW WHAT?"

You're going to narrow the subject, so focus in on just what aspect you'll write about.

If the task seems too big, agree that for now you'll do only the ten-minute writing suggested below, simply as a warm-up, for the sheer good feeling of putting words on paper.

Write your subject in CAPITAL LETTERS across the top of a page, and leave it.

Open with your relaxation exercise (p. 13).

Start Anywhere, Keep Talking on Paper	When you open your eyes, read what's on the page and simply start anywhere. Double space. Pretend you're telling a story to a friend. Talk it out. Don't worry about paragraphs, awkward places, spelling: just keep going! You'll shape it later. Talk about the subject or (to keep the pen or carriage moving) about your sense impressions now. Don't grope for the right word: keep writing. Good!
Double Space	
Keep Going!	

Try for two pages, and stop.

Notice that when writing this way you're never stuck. You don't start from any particular point, but can *begin anew with any sentence.*

Now you're in motion. Time to focus in.

UNDERLINE anything that strikes you, that hits the mark.

FIND A QUESTION in these highlights. Be specific. Ask yourself what, how, or why . . . ?

Perhaps you want to describe your pet project. Ask yourself: What's this project about, and who'll benefit?

Try Experiment 48.

■■■■

Experiment 48
Ask your question,[2] answer freely

---

1. Write or type your question, with question mark, across the top of the page, and leave it.
2. Relax from head to toe.
3. WRITE NONSTOP whatever comes to you. Trust that answers

---

[2] Such as: "What have I done that they'd want to hear about?" "How can we sell more shoes?" "Have women been discriminated against throughout history?" "What's this project about, and who'll benefit?"

will appear once you're in motion. "Talk" on paper. Start anew with any sentence. Keep going.

4. Read over what you've written, and underline highlights, anything that "hits the mark."

You've got momentum. Repeat Experiment 48 with another question, more specific than the first. When you have a lot of material, go on to Experiment 49.

Did you notice
—a few surprisingly well-turned phrases?
—that things are bubbling up in you now?
—you've managed to get some good ideas into words on paper?
—you've found a painless way to get going, to push your own start button?

You've tried Experiment 48, and you have pages with underlinings, and perhaps some notes as well. "This must be where the hard part comes in," you'll probably say.

But getting going and generating ideas is the hard part and now something's about to take shape!

Let Experiment 49 help you produce a working draft of the whole piece.

Experiment 49
Talk in paragraphs: What's the story?

Arrange
Highlights
on a "Main
Points" Sheet

1. Read over underlinings and notes. Arrange highlights as a list of main points, numbering according to what you should say first, next, last. If the order isn't clear to you yet, do you see a NATURAL STARTING POINT? Begin there for now.

"So What's It All About?

2. Imagine talking with a friend who asks, "So what's it all about?" Begin at the beginning, and "tell" her straight out. "Talk" in paragraphs. Double space this.

"Talk" in Paragraphs

3. Begin a new paragraph each time you shift gears, bringing in a new idea, or intensifying what you said last. Paragraphs can be short. You can leave space on the page if you haven't got all the facts to feed in yet. The point is to keep going. Stick to "one paragraph, one aspect."

One Paragraph, One Aspect

"And So?" New Paragraph

Each paragraph moves the piece forward. When there's a lull (you're not sure where to go next), it's as if your friend asks, "And so?"

Keep Going!

New paragraph. "Talk" out on paper everything you can.

Feed in All Your Highlights

4. Spread pages with underlinings around you so they catch your eye, and can feed your writing. Later, you'll tighten, sharpen, rearrange, correct. Now, just concentrate on developing as many ideas as you can, and getting them down on paper.

Briefly List Points You'll Get to

5. If, as you're writing, a flurry of points you want to cover occurs to you, take only a minute to jot them down on your "main points sheet." Then get back to the idea you're developing.

Keep on "Talking" in Paragraphs

When you run out of steam for a moment, look to your "main points sheet," and take up the next item that logically follows from the one you just wrote. "Talk" in paragraphs about the next main point you feel you can write about now.

Feed in from All Your Sources

6. When you need to check something (find a quotation, a statistic, or a book), go ahead. Your essay is building now: this is your first draft, so feed in as much as you can.

Check Your Main Points Sheet

7. What do you need to say next? Check off each point on your list. Have you covered everything?

Read Your Opening; Tie In, Sum Up

8. Read your opening. You want your final words to tiein. Can you sum up in a sentence or two what this piece is about?

*   *   *

Congratulations! You've come a long way from that blank sheet of paper.

Rearrange

If you want to work a little more on this draft, look for sentences and paragraphs that obviously fit better in an earlier or later place. Don't bother retyping now. Just cut up and rearrange, or use your computer to move blocks of text, as if you were fitting together the pieces of a puzzle. Place parts into the order that's easiest to follow.

Let It Rest if You're Tired

Important: If you're tired, let it rest for now. You'll see "what fits where" much more clearly when you take a fresh look later.

TIP: Remember to save all drafts on the computer.

Did you notice
  —*momentum helps you write? that it's useful to start writing rather than thinking about it?*
  —*you had more to say than you thought before you started?*
  —*that writing about one idea stimulated other ideas?*

To sum up:

SEVEN STEPS TO HELP YOU WRITE

1. *Write a question you want to answer.*
2. *Relax from head to toe.*
3. *"Talk" nonstop on paper.*
4. *Underline highlights.*
5. *Arrange a main points list.*
6. *"Talk" in paragraphs: what's the story?*
7. *Rest, then revise.*

GIVE YOURSELF AN ENCOURAGING WORD

Whenever you're pleased by what you wrote, like now when you have a first draft, take a minute at the height of your enthusiasm to make yourself a sign or note expressing how you feel. Look at it when you doubt what you've done is any good. We all need an encouraging word.

THIS MAKES GOOD READING!
KEEP GOING!

TEN THINGS TO TRY WHEN YOU'RE STUCK

You're in the middle of writing something, or you want to start, and notice inner resistance, in the form of the thought: "I can't, I don't want to, I don't know how to get this part right. . . ." That's your signal to . . .

TAKE A VACATION! Create a new condition in yourself, in your body. Get the juices flowing and find new energy for your writing.

Try any of these activities as an experiment, see if they help you start fresh.

1. Talk, talk, talk! about what you're writing. It gets you excited again, and emotion means more energy. When ideas and phrases start coming, jot them down, then write nonstop.

2. If you jog, RUN. When you feel exhilarated, start typing what

you want to say as fast as you can. Watch a page come pouring out.

3. Shower or sauna, especially trying to be aware of the surface of your skin. Whenever a discouraging thought occurs to you about what you're writing, simply sense the skin you're in: water on it, air on it, face, behind the knees. Later, write just one paragraph.

4. Dance up a sweat to your favorite music, whatever gets your body moving. Right away, ask yourself a question on paper, and answer it, writing quickly. Start anew with any sentence.

5. Charged up by good news? Now's the time to sit at the typewriter and do that part of your writing you've been putting off. All that energy will get you going strong.

6. Write your subject across the top of the page. Below it write: "What's the story?" Put aside pad and pen, or move your chair away from the computer. DO THE RELAXATION EXERCISE (p. 13) for five minutes. Then write nonstop to the bottom of the page.

7. Lie down, your back and the soles of your feet flat on the floor, knees up, head raised just a few inches on a pillow or book. In this resting position, sense the whole length of your spine along the floor. IMAGINE you're breathing in through different parts of your body, as if air could come in through your abdomen . . . scalp. . . . When you feel refreshed, try Experiment 48.

8. Take a walk. Let thoughts about writing remind you simply to become aware of each foot contacting the ground. SIT down with pad, and make a list of the points you want to cover in the piece you're writing.

9. Do any favorite activity that invigorates, yoga, stretching exercises, or aerobics. Return again and again to the sensation of your body. Later, write a question you want to answer and pick up your favorite pen (the one that has a nice "feel" as the ink flows onto the page): handwrite line after line.

10. Paint, pot, weave, sew, knit; repair or clean up something, trying to be aware, moment to moment, of the contact of hand and object. Start writing as if the whole story is there already, waiting to come out.

TIP: IF YOU'RE STUCK AT A PARTICULAR PLACE, sometimes you can ask yourself: What bothers me about this part? What does this piece need now? Write your response!

Trust that, with practice, you'll be clever and patient enough to get by any block. Make a pact with yourself that you'll never "force things" but instead will:

1. Recognize when you need a break and fresh energy.
2. Practice creating a new condition in yourself.
3. Try an experiment: write any first sentence or question just to get going.

The more you see how you can overcome being stuck, the more confident you become that you can write anything you want. You've done it once, and you'll do it again!

BECOMING
YOUR
OWN
BEST
EDITOR

Talking in paragraphs brought out your unmistakable voice: the writing has drive and strength that comes from your natural way of expressing things. Your writing lives! and you're not about to formalize it to death.

You want only to tighten and sharpen what you have.

But how? If you're feeling it's going to be a chore, this is *not* the moment to begin, right? Set aside the work for a while. Come back when you're so curious you just have to take a look at all those pages you wrote.

And as you do it, is there something you'd like to cross out? After hours of restraint, you may be eager to play editor. You see that this part sags, that you use a word too much, that another part sounds too . . .

Editing can be such a relief! Now's your chance to unburden every sentence. Cross out without regret. The ultimate satisfaction comes when you type the final draft and feel you've got the exact words you want in the best order.

So, what stays and what goes?

"But everything looks good."

While you're learning what to look for, rather than trying to do everything at once, you can read over your piece three times in this way:

1st reading: Listen for tone, locate rough spots.

2nd reading: Notice how you get from here to there.

3rd reading: Tighten and sharpen.

And, when you've got a sentence that's convoluted and confusing, try Experiment 50 ("Say it over coffee").

FIRST: LISTEN FOR TONE, LOCATE ROUGH SPOTS

IMAGINE YOU'RE AN EDITOR, not the writer of this piece, and you're seeing it for the first time. It's your job to carve out the best of what's here.

Read Out Loud

READ PAGE ONE OUT LOUD to someone because you'll hear more. Ask your listener to answer these three questions (you may be able to answer them yourself):

—What part do you remember? (Good!)

What Stands Out?

—What part do you need to hear again (didn't quite catch)? (Revise?)

What Tone?

—In a few words, how does the voice coming through sound? (Sincere, informed? hedging? confused? boring? argumentative?)

What Purpose?

Decide on the purpose of this piece so you can check for appropriate tone of voice. Does the writing entertain or inform you? Try to get someone to do something? And if you're that someone, ideally what tone of voice would reach *you*?

TRY TO IDENTIFY WHICH WORDS defeat that purpose: what group of words nags at you a little as you read? Usually you can hear rough spots the moment you say them aloud to someone.

Cross out or
Bracket []
What Bothers
You

Don't labor over these places now, unless you see right away what to omit or change. Just cross out in pencil, or bracket what bothers you. Write TK (to come) in the margin, and go on.

Who's Your
Audience?

While reading for tone of voice and rough spots, you can also keep in mind whom the piece is written for. A group of businessmen? An English teacher? Does it sound casual or formal? WHAT PRONOUN suits this piece?

For example, the reader of a formal report might respond better to a less "personal" tone. Go through and strike out all instances of "I'm writing this to," "I think," "You can see." Instead of *I* and *you,* use *one* and (the "editorial") *we:*

One finds striking examples of . . .
We read that computers are . . .

In this way, turn casual remarks into strong declarative sentences which make your opinion sound as if it's the reasonable point of view.

WHAT PRONOUN WORKS BEST?

If you're writing	Try:	Example:
a "how to" article	you	First, you want to see . . .
an after-dinner speech	I, we	I saw we needed to try . . .
a paper for school	one	One finds in Emerson's . . .
a technical report	one	One accounts for such . . .
a story	I, he, she	I waited, but she never . . .

Stick with whatever pronoun works best and check to be sure you don't switch (from "I saw" to "You could see") halfway through the paragraph (see p. 10).

Did you notice any vague places, or clichés? For instance, you're talking about some historical event and write, "and they got mad and did something about it." Isn't it vague? Who did what, specifically?

You can write TK in the margin, and sharpen these places later. If you want to improve them now, supply specifics.

Vague? Turn pronouns into nouns (names of persons, places, or things).

Check facts, dates, and the spellings of proper nouns.

Clichés? About clichés: in your haste it was easy to write "too funny for words." How funny? Look up *funny* in a thesaurus. Or show how people reacted.

Or you wrote: "We took everything but the kitchen sink." What's everything? "We took *Supply* sleeping bags, rafts, insect repellent, charcoal *Specifics* briquets, and a baseball bat."

Unless you're deliberately using clichés and vague phrases (to characterize a particular person who's speaking), give specifics.

SECOND: CHECK OUT YOUR BEGINNING, MIDDLE, END, AND LINKS BETWEEN PARTS

Beginning
—First sentence: ho-hum or tell-me-more?
—Start farther along (where it heats up)?
—Does the reader know soon enough what it's about?
    Too soon? (Spoils the suspense)
    Too late? (Not sure, can't be bothered)

Middle
—Moving forward briskly? Going somewhere?
—Easy to follow? One paragraph, one aspect?
—Where does it sag, slow down, or stop?
    What if you cross out that whole part?
    Clearer?

CHECK YOUR ORDER OF PRESENTATION

1. *In pencil in the margin next to each paragraph JOT DOWN A FEW KEY WORDS that tell the main point.*

2. *Does any sentence in that paragraph not apply? Omit, or move it?*

   To move a sentence, circle and mark it with a letter ("A"). Then write "INSERT A" where that sentence fits better.

3. *On a separate page, list your margin jottings. Does each point lead to the next?*

   To move a paragraph, circle and mark it with a letter ("X"). Then write "INSERT X" where that paragraph belongs.

End

—Satisfying? Worth the time it takes?
—Is it clear why the piece is written?
—Does it leave you with a strong impression? What's that?
—Is this the place to stop? Gone on too long? Anti-climactic?
—Does the ending relate to the beginning?

Here are some ways to link paragraphs so your piece holds together and moves well:

1. REPEAT A KEY WORD you used in Paragraph A when you write the opener for Paragraph B.
2. OPEN a paragraph with the next question in your reader's mind. Use a question mark.
3. USE A TRANSITIONAL word or phrase *unless the reader can follow* perfectly well without it. PREPARE your reader for what's coming:

an example:	For instance
	For example,
a shift:	However,
	But
	Nevertheless,
	Or
	Up to this point
a reason:	Because,
	Therefore,
	In order to
another reason:	In addition,
	Also,
	Moreover,
a comparison:	Similarly,
	In the same way,
	In the same vein,
a contrast:	In contrast,
	Contrary to
	However,
	Unlike
another time:	Before
	Afterward,
	Then
a sequence:	First,
	Second,
	Third,
	Next,
a conclusion:	Thus,
	Therefore,
	To sum up,

NOTICE HOW YOU GET FROM HERE TO THERE

COHERENCE: Does one sentence lead naturally into the next? Can you easily follow from one paragraph to the next? Enough tie-ins and transitions? Something developing or building?

EMPHASIS: Are you rambling on, or do you show the relative importance of ideas? Is your main point clear? Does it stand out?

UNITY: Are you on a straight line from the beginning, through the middle, to the end? Do you keep to one purpose? Are you still writing in your natural voice?

THIRD: TIGHTEN AND SHARPEN

Tightening and sharpening, taking out some words and substituting others: this is your final task. You've located rough spots, places that just don't sit well with you, sentences you want to improve with one aim in mind: to make your meaning clear.

Does each word pull its weight? What effect are you trying for? What may seem like flowery language may suit a parody. The fewest words, in plain English, may make a stronger letter. Every sentence, every word, should strengthen what you're saying.

So look for words, phrases, and sentences you can do without. When in doubt, cross it out, or at least experiment, listening to that section without those words. Do you like it better? Does it move well?

WHAT NEEDS TIGHTENING?

* Do I need these words?
* Is my writing better without them?

To practice becoming your own best editor, LOOK for the following places in your writing, and CIRCLE. Suggestions for revising are in parentheses after each example.

—repeated words, phrases, ideas:
"he has never succeeded and always fails"   ("he always fails")

"let's *cooperate together* on this"   ("let's cooperate")

"we *first began* the project"   ("we began")

"generate ideas and generate enthusiasm" ("generate ideas and enthusiasm")

—that, which, who:

"in spite of the fact that she is a woman who" ("although she")

—extra, little words:

"meets with our approval" ("we approve")

"we are writing to ask that you send" ("please send")

"due to the fact that" ("because")

—jargon

"enclosed herewith please find" ("enclosed is"; "here's")

"in the event that" ("if")

"effectuate the implementation of" ("implement" or "act on")

—jumbles of words which make you say "what?":
"Probably we should reconsider the assignment of control responsibilities as the proper development of guidelines for controls must reside with the most closely associated professional representative. . . ." (Try Experiment 50!)

—dull verbs, one after another (is it monotonous?): "There is no doubt that it is time for it to become a reality" ("It's time")

—energetic verbs, one after another (is it too much?): "Come here," he bellowed, and then chortled, "you cutie." She wheezed, "I can't," then admonished, "Don't come closer." (Use these verbs sparingly unless trying for a comic effect)

—adjectives and adverbs, too abundant (it is too flowery?):
"Immaculately white sailboats glided smoothly and gracefully in stately majestic procession" (what words can you cut?)

Now that you've noticed some rough spots, cut out every word you don't need: is the sentence clearer?

If you're concerned about wordiness, here are some examples of extra words you can cut from your writing. In each instance, which word is unnecessary?

honest truth
true facts
color green
rules and regulations
small in size
assemble together
cooperate together
scrutinize carefully
enclosed you will find
narrow in width

necessary requirement
first began
postpone until later
hour of noon
pair of twins
fall down
refer back
city of Hartford
advance planning
from a northeast direction

Tightening your writing means cutting out words you don't need. Look over each sentence as if you want to put it in the fewest words. Don't be attached to any word or phrase if you have an inkling you'd be better off if you cut it.

These are not rules to follow arbitrarily, just places to look when you want to revise. Remember you're still experimenting: do you like your tightened version better? Does it ring true to your experience or idea?

You notice the meaning may change when you rearrange. Perhaps your original sentence, with all those words, has a rhythm that expresses perfectly what you mean. Leave it. Context is crucial: when what's on the page suits your meaning, you already may have "the best words in the best order." For instance. You repeat a phrase, but each time change it slightly. "Repeat and vary" can be powerful, as in these final lines from Walt Whitman's "Song of the Open Road":

Allons! the road is before us!
It is safe—I have tried it—my own feet have
    tried it well—be not detain'd!

Let the paper remain on the desk unwritten, and
    the book on the shelf unopen'd!
Let the tools remain in the workshop! let the
    money remain unearn'd!

Let the school stand! mind not the cry of the teacher!
Let the preacher preach in his pulpit! let the lawyer plead in
the court, and the judge expound the law.

Camerado, I give you my hand!
I give you my love more precious than money,
I give you myself before preaching or law;
Will you give me yourself? will you come travel with me?
Shall we stick by each other as long as we live?

WHAT NEEDS SHARPENING?

Circle the following words in your writing and see if
revising helps.

—*is, was, were* (forms of the verb "to be" used too often)
Here's how to switch to the "active" voice:

	"Active" verbs
sounds could be heard →	we *heard* sounds
it is important to study	one *should study*
there is no problem	no problem *exists*

Note: You need not omit every instance of "it is" or
"there is." In a scientific report, you may prefer to use
them to avoid "I" (see p. 138).

—dull verbs, such as *go, move, have, make*
If you're writing a story especially, look up your
"dull" verb in a thesaurus. *Go* might yield *shuffle,
limp, saunter, strut.* Does one of these suit the passage?

Instead of: This room has the look of a deserted barn.
Write: This room *looks* like . . .
Instead of: He moved with difficulty into the room.
Write: He *hobbled* into the room.

Note: Don't overdo (see p. 120 about too many "dynamic" verbs).

—colorless phrases which explain rather than show

Instead of: He was feeling rather bad.
Show it: He slumped in his chair.

Show by means of posture, movement, gesture.

—"hedge" words: sort of, kind of, possibly, somewhat, relatively

Instead of: Terry was sort of a saint to me, and somewhat of an influence on me in a relatively short time.
Write: I idolized Terry; in a short time, she changed my life.
Take the risk of sounding sure. Is it stronger?

—negative phrases ("did not") when you could find a stronger positive phrasing

Instead of: He did not have much confidence in books on writing, and did not think them very useful.
Try this: He *distrusted* books on writing, and thought them *useless*.

Experiment 50
Sounds confusing? Say it over coffee

When you're not sure how to revise a confusing or wordy sentence, try this with someone:

1. READ ALOUD the sentence you want to make clear. LOOK UP.
2. Your friend asks, "What do you mean?"

3. SAY "I MEAN . . ." and say what you mean straight out. (*Don't* look down at the page.)
4. WRITE down what you just said—that's it! Try it (or something like it) in the passage.

Did you notice
   —*that looking at the page, and moving words around, some-times doesn't help you make the passage clearer?*
   —*how useful it is simply to lift your head, and "talk out" just what you mean?*
   —*that when you tell someone what you mean, you say it simply and clearly?*

A QUICK CHECKLIST

Wordy	*Cut out extra words?*
or	*Say it just once?*
Concise?	*Suits your meaning?*
Active	*Too many "it is" and "there is"?*
Verbs or	*"We heard them" (active) or "they could be*
Passive?	*heard" (passive)—which works best?*
Jargon or	*Say it in two words instead of eight?*
Plain	*easily understood?*
English?	*Would you "say it over coffee".*
Show	*Vivid sensory details?*
or	*Concrete specifics and telling examples?*
Explain?	*Energetic verbs?*
Flows	*Logical progression from here to there?*
or	*Clear transitions so you can follow easily?*
Falters?	*Any leaps or gaps?*

WHEN TO PROOFREAD, AND WHY IT PAYS

You've been working for hours and have read each page so many times you don't notice typos or spelling mistakes. LET IT REST for a while! You need to come to it with new eyes.

When you're ready to proofread, look at each sentence. There's no hurry. Remember you owe it to the quality of your work to catch those errors in spelling, typing, punctuation, and grammar. Minor mistakes distract your reader, make her lose faith in you as someone worth reading. Even a penciled-in correction is better than an error.

How does the page look? Adequate margins? Not crammed, but easy to read?

Look at each sentence for spelling, typos, and punctuation.

—CHECK A DICTIONARY to spell any word you're not sure of.

—CHECK A GRAMMAR HANDBOOK to find out what's correct.

Which spelling do you mean for a sound-alike, *principle* or *principal*? *Affect* or *effect*? What is the past tense of *lie*? *Lay, laid,* or *lain*? Where does the apostrophe go in "Jones's house"?

When you come to the end of a line, how do you divide a word correctly? Break it where? See a dictionary.

If you know you are a poor speller, **always use the spell-checker on your computer.**

If you're not sure about any of the terms in the checklist below, read the section which follows ("What About Spelling, Punctuation, and Grammar?").

PROOFREADER'S CHECKLIST

Consult a HANDBOOK of English or a DICTIONARY as needed.

GRAMMAR

❑ Where are there sentence fragments, fused sentences, comma splices, and misplaced modifiers?

❑ Are there any sentences in which subject, verb, and pronoun do not agree in number (e.g., plural subject but singular pronoun referring to it)?

PUNCTUATION AND CAPITALIZATION

❑ Does a question end with a question mark?

❑ Do all the proper names, and the main words of the title, begin with capital letters?

❑ Are the names of books and newspapers underlined (or italicized)?

❑ Are the names of stories, essays, articles, and poems in quotation marks?

❑ Are quotation marks used around the exact words of a speaker?

Are they set off (preceded) by a comma or colon?

Is the period inside the ending quotation marks?

❑ Are short quotations (from people and literature) placed inside quotation marks?

Are longer quotations (three or more lines) blocked five spaces in from both margins (with no quotation marks)?

❑ Do all possessives and contractions have the necessary apostrophes?

Are apostrophes in the right place? (e.g., Do you mean *it's* or *its*?)

❑ Is the semicolon used correctly?

❑ Have comma splices been corrected (so a comma is NOT used between complete sentences)?

SPELLING AND TYPOS

❑ Have you identified every word that looks misspelled?

❑ Have you checked "sound-alikes" (e.g., *there, their, they're; conscious, conscience*) to see if the word meant is correctly spelled?

GOOD WORK!

WHAT ABOUT SPELLING, PUNCTUATION, AND GRAMMAR?

SOME COMMON MISTAKES TO WATCH FOR

Spelling

IT'S or ITS?	→ IT'S always means IT IS
	(Memorize: It's time for its bath)
YOU'RE or YOUR?	→ YOU'RE always means YOU ARE
THEY'RE,	→ THEY'RE always means THEY ARE
THEIR,	→ as in "their book" (whose?)
THERE?	→ as in "over there" (where?)
A LOT	→ is two words

Punctuation

If you're not sure when to use a comma or semicolon, look in a handbook for the rule. Watch for these places:

1. Don't put a comma between subject and verb.

   WRONG: Another fantasy of mine, is to . . .
   → RIGHT: Another fantasy of mine is to . . .

2. Don't use only a comma when you need a stronger "stop" between two long complete sentences.[1]

   WRONG: I was confident about meeting him, I'd heard he was
              sympathetic.
   → RIGHT: I was confident about meeting him. I'd heard he was
              sympathetic.

   (or)

           I was confident about meeting him; I'd heard . . .

   If you have a series of short, complete sentences, you can use commas, such as:
   → RIGHT: I paced, I wept, I moaned.

---

[1] A complete sentence has a *subject* (person, place, or thing) and a verb (shows action or state of being). The verb form "agrees" with the subject (that is, both singular or both plural).

    The *book* is finished. *John* ran home. (*You*) Watch it!
    s.   v.   s.   v.   s.   v.

3. Don't run together two complete sentences when you need a "stop" between them. (Put in a period, semicolon, or colon, *not* a comma.) Correct fused sentences and comma splices.

HOW TO LOCATE AND CORRECT A COMMA SPLICE

EXAMPLE OF A "COMMA SPLICE"

WRONG: *The widgets sold out, however more will be available soon.*

Note that you have two complete sentences, each of which could stand alone: *The widgets sold out* and *More will be available soon.*

When you have two complete sentences, each of which can stand alone, be sure to place a *period* or *semicolon* between them—NOT a comma.

THREE WAYS TO CORRECT COMMA SPLICES

- *Place a period at the end of the first sentence, and capitalize the first word of the second sentence. (OR)*

- *Place a semicolon between the sentences. (OR)*

- *Place a comma and a coordinating conjunction ("and" "or" "but") between sentences.*

EXAMPLE OF A COMMA SPLICE

WRONG: *The widgets sold out, however more will be available soon.*

EXAMPLE CORRECTED THREE WAYS

*The widgets sold **out. However,** more will be available soon.*

*The widgets sold **out; however,** more will be available soon.*

*The widgets sold **out, but** more will be available soon.*

---

4. Place the apostrophe correctly when you have TWO NOUNS TOGETHER to show possessives (*corporation's records*).

Singular Possessives:

a. If the first noun is singular, add apostrophe + *s*
   dog's collar (the collar of one dog)
   Chris's pencils (the pencils of one person named Chris)

Plural Possessives:

b. If the first noun is plural and ends in *s*, add the apostrophe after the *s*
   cats' kennel (the kennel of several cats)
   teachers' association (the association of several teachers)

c. If the first noun is plural and does NOT end in *s*, add apostrophe + *s*
   children's zoo (the zoo for the children)
   men's teams (the teams made up of men)

NOTE: DON'T use an apostrophe to show possession with PRONOUNS. Possessive pronouns indicate possession by their spelling alone: *his book, theirs are accurate, ours need more work.*

Here's a Style Sheet for Apostrophes. Check it when you're not sure where to place an apostrophe.

A STYLE SHEET FOR APOSTROPHES

Singular Possessives:
> *child's toys*
> *a day's effort*
> *Mr. Benson's house*
> *Mrs. Jones's house*
> *this season's fashions*
> *anyone's problems*
> *Chris's report*
> *the Chairman of the Board's decision*

185

> *his mother-in-law's request*
> *Anderson and Shaw's article*
>   (one article)
> *Anderson's and Shaw's promotions*
>   (two promotions)
>
> Plural Possessives:
>   Nouns ending in *s*:
>   *writers' conference*
>   *40 days' notice*
>   *the Joneses' house*
>
>   Nouns not ending in *s*:
>   *women's opportunities*
>   *children's books*
>   *the men's room*
>   *oxen's yoke*
>
> Contractions, Missing Letters, and Other:
>   *We'd (we would), don't (do not), can't (cannot), it's (it is)*
>   *would've (would have), I've (I have), aren't (are not)*
>   *How many i's in the word "liaison"?*
>   *He knows his ABC's.*
>   *Spirit of '76*
>   *the '60s (the sixties)*

Grammar and sentence structure

Check for these:

☐ "Danglers" (the phrase you open with is not close enough to the word it describes: confusion results). These are "misplaced modifiers."

WRONG: *Hiding his nuts in the tree, John watched the squirrel.* (Who hid what?)

→ RIGHT: John watched the squirrel hiding his nuts in the tree.

WRONG: Swimming in the sea, the waves nearly drowned us. (Were the waves swimming?)

→ RIGHT: *Swimming* in the sea, *we* nearly drowned in the waves.

Whenever you begin a sentence with an "—ing" phrase, be sure the word coming right after the comma is the person or thing that's hurrying, swimming, or hiding.

Watch for places where you need to PUT RELATED WORDS CLOSE TOGETHER, next to each other.

☐ "Modifiers" (adjectives and adverbs) not close enough to the word they modify or describe

WRONG: He only found two arrowheads.

→ RIGHT: He found *only two* arrowheads. (How many? Only two.)

☐ Subject so far from the verb it's confusing

UNCLEAR: The boys wanting to see a deer and hoping that if they walked very quietly would not scare away the animals put on their sneakers.

→ CLEAR: The boys put on their sneakers. They wanted . . .

☐ Sentence fragments (You can use an incomplete sentence for effect. Otherwise, try to write complete sentences.)

INCOMPLETE: The wedding present that got him started in pottery. (Verb missing: what did the present *do*? what about it?)

→ COMPLETE: The wedding present got him started in pottery.

☐ Lack of "agreement" among subject, verb, and possessive pronoun (all singular? all plural?)

WRONG: Everyone has their problems.
(with labels above: s. over "Everyone", v. over "has", pron. over "their")

(*Everyone* is singular, but *their* is plural).

→ RIGHT: People have their problems.

Writing quickly, we make this mistake a lot, especially with the words *everybody, anybody, no one, nobody*. Usually, all take a singular verb (has, goes, is) and a singular possessive pronoun (*his, her*). To avoid sexist language (*his, her*), make subject and pronouns plural (*they, their*). There are exceptions. When the word referred to is plural in *meaning* (although singular in form), it can take a plural pronoun:

→ RIGHT: Everybody was at the party, and *they* all stayed late to sing *their* songs.

To check for agreement do you need to locate the subject, verb, and pronoun? Ignore intervening prepositional phrases.

Try this:

Cross out phrases beginning *"to the _____ , in the _____ ,"* *"of . . ."*
(with labels: preposition over "to", prep. over "in", prep. over "of")

Find the verb. If the subject is singular, is the verb?
Memorize: *Each* of the girls has her own room.
(with labels: s. over "Each", prep. phrase over "of the girls")

("each, has, her": all singular)

☐ Lack of parallelism when using combinations such as either . . . or . . . ," "both . . . and . . . ," "not only . . . but also"[2]

WRONG: Either you find an example or weaken your case.

→ RIGHT: You either find an example or weaken your case.

---

[2]coordinating conjunctions

Check what part of speech (verb, noun, pronoun?) comes directly after *either* and after *or*. Try for the same part of speech:

> either *verb*   Either *find* . . . (v.)
> or   *verb*   or *weaken* . . .

WRONG: You not only should check punctuation but also grammar. (v.)

RIGHT: You should check not only punctuation but also grammar.

> not only *noun* . . . not only *punctuation*. (n.)
> but also *noun*   but also *grammar*. (n.)

Here's one more example of KEEPING THINGS PARALLEL.

WRONG: I can show you how *to get* going, how *to carry* on, how *to revise*, and *punctuation*. (three verbs and a noun)

→ RIGHT: I can show you how *to get* going, how *to carry* on, how *to revise*, and how *to punctuate*.

→ EVEN BETTER (TIGHTENED): I can show you how to get going, carry on, revise, and punctuate. (four verbs in parallel form)

If these common mistakes and ways to correct them are totally unfamiliar, you may need to improve your writing skills. Study a composition handbook with the answers in the back, such as *The Least You Should Know About English*.

APPRECIATE YOUR FINAL DRAFT

You did it! And you can do it again.

What a wealth of material you've put together. Your persistence paid off. Doesn't it feel good to finish something?

Congratulations. Now, treat yourself: CELEBRATE!

Glossary

ABSTRACT. (1) n. A summary giving the main points. (2) adj. Theoretical, general, indefinite (rather than concrete and specific), such as a concept, or a quality apart from a particular object (e.g., blackness, freedom, honesty).

ARGUMENT. A reason offered for or against something. A proof designed to persuade.

BIBLIOGRAPHY. An alphabetical list of all books and articles read or consulted, including but not limited to those appearing in footnotes. A *bibliography* always goes at the end of a paper under the title Works Cited.

The correct form for a book is as follows:

Author's Last Name, First Name. *Book*. City of publication: Publisher, year.

Here's a sample list, in alphabetical order, as it would appear at the end of a document.

WORKS CITED

Anderson, Simon. "Future Trends in Fiber Optics."
    Electronics and Technology Today 27 (19--): 10–20.
Baker, Bronson. *Fiber Optics: The Future of the Indus-
    try.* New York: Petersen Publishing Company,
    19--.
––––––. "Fiber Optics Now!" *Time* 8 Feb. 19--:
    82–64.
Caldwell, A. W. *Studies in Fiber Optics.* 2 vols.
    Philadelphia: Big Books Press, 19--.
Freedman, P., and Paul Johnson. *The History of Fiber
    Optics.* Berkeley: Innovative Books, 19--.

In the first item above (*Anderson*), the author is Simon
Anderson (last name, comma, first name), with a period after
the name. His article is "Future Trends in Fiber Optics" in
quotation marks. Notice that you put the period *inside* the
quotation marks. Next comes the italicized or underlined
title of the journal in which the article is found.

Then comes the volume number with no punctuation
after it, followed by the parenthesis with the date of publication (*19--*). Follow the second parentheses with a colon,
space, and the page numbers on which the article appears.
Whenever you go to additional lines, indent them five
spaces from the left margin. End with a period.

The second item above (*Baker*) is the typical citation for
a book.

The third item above (another work by Baker) refers to
an article by Baker in a weekly magazine. You need not
repeat the author's name but use instead three hyphens
followed by a period.

For a *weekly* magazine, note the way the date is cited (*8
Feb. 19--*), giving day, month, and year. For a *monthly*
magazine, you'd give the month but not the day.

The fourth item above (*Caldwell*) is the citation for a work in two volumes, as indicated.

The fifth item (*Freedman*) cites a book with two authors. Notice that for the second author (*Paul Johnson*), you *don't* put the last name first. The same holds true for a third author (use first name, then last).

CAUSE AND EFFECT. *Cause* refers to the reason something happened. *Effect* refers to the result of what happened. For example:

>   His harsh words made her cry.
>   cause   effect

CHARACTER. A being, person, or individual in a story.

CHARACTERIZATION. The creation of an imaginary person or being. *Characterization* provides details of posture, gesture, speech, actions, thoughts, physical appearance, reactions, wishes, and dreams.

CLIMAX. The turning point in a story, when something is resolved.

CONCRETE. adj. Tangible, specific, perceivable to the senses. *Concrete* details have to do with actual things or events. Some *concrete* details are: a dripping faucet, a red poinsettia, cinnamon toast, peacock feathers.

CONFLICT. The meeting of opposing forces or persons. *Conflict* involves a battle for mastery, a clash of personalities, interests, opinions, ideals, or goals.

CONTEXT. Words, phrases, or sentences coming before and after a given passage. These words, phrases, or sentences throw light on the meaning of the passage.

CRISIS. A crucial or decisive moment in a struggle when things change for better or worse. A *crisis* leads to the climax.

DESCRIPTION. A *description* shows how something looks, sounds, smells, tastes, feels to the touch, and conveys a picture or impression through the use of sensory specifics; vivid pertinent details are selected and shaped for a certain effect.

DIALOGUE. A conversation; a spoken exchange of ideas, feelings, and information. *Dialogue* reveals characters, and advances the action of a story.

DISSERTATION. A formal essay or thesis treating a subject extensively.

DOCUMENTATION. Supporting material or evidence, cited in footnotes and listed in a bibliography, to back up statements.

EDITORIAL WE. The use of the pronoun *we* instead of *I* in reports, speeches, and letters (e.g., "We at Con Oil feel a responsibility to . . .").

EFFECTIVENESS. Getting the results you want, creating the desired impression. *Effectiveness* requires communicating in a clear way.

EMPHASIS. Stressing an idea or word to show its importance.

EMPHASIZING. Making something stand out.

EXPOSITION. Explaining something, defining or analyzing it, in an essay.

FICTION. An imagined or invented composition or story that never happened.

FLASHBACK (1) n. A scene or incident that happened earlier. (2) vb. To *flashback* is to go from the present moment to a prior time.

FOOTNOTE. A listing of information about any document cited in your essay. Direct quotations, someone else's ideas, and passages from others' works must be footnoted when you cite them as examples and supporting material. *Footnotes* go at the bottom of the page on which the material is used, or as a list of "Notes" at the end of the paper. Indent the first line like this:

[1]Fran Shaw, *50 Ways to Help You Write* (Stamford: Longmeadow Press, 1995), p. 125.

Instead of using footnotes, the Modern Language Association recommends using *in-text notes* (which refer to a list of Works Cited at the end of a paper). A *signal phrase* within your sentence identifies the **author**, and all you need do is put the page **number** from the source in parenthesis, like this:

> According to **Matthiessen,** Wordsworth suffered "a great falling off in genius" in his later years **(225).**

Or simply use the author's last **name** and the page **number** in parentheses, like this:

> Whitman "is America . . . his time and his people" **(Pound, 8).**

See page 147 ("Citing Sources") or consult the Documentation section of any current handbook of English with rules for writers, such as Diana Hacker's *A Writer's Reference.*

HAIKU. A Japanese poem of seventeen syllables. A *haiku* expresses a heightened moment of awareness.

HERO or HEROINE. Usually the main character in a story, possessing some special quality, strength, or ability.

IMAGE. A likeness of something or someone. An *image* vividly represents physical characteristics or a quality of life (e.g., a man might be described as "a great lumbering bear," a woman's eyes as "pools of light").

INDEX. An alphabetical list of topics discussed in a book. An *index* appears at the back of a book with page numbers showing where the topics appear.

JARGON. The vocabulary of a special group or profession. A special private language, not common speech. *Jargon* can also mean unintelligible language (gobbledygook, gibberish, "business-ese," "legal-ese"). The following phrase is an example of *jargon:* "endeavor to ascertain what was heretofore deemed unobtainable."

JOURNAL. A daily, personal record of what happened, what you read and thought or felt.

MOOD. The prevailing emotional state, atmosphere, or tone in a piece of writing. *Mood* is conveyed through selected details of what a character sees or thinks or feels.

MOTIVATION. Why a character does what he does. *Motivations* are the causes, reasons, explanations supplied to show what drives a character.

NARRATION, NARRATIVE. An account of what happened.

NONFICTION. Writing based on facts and reality. *Nonfiction* is not imagined or invented. Examples of non-fictional writing are autobiography, biography, science, and history books.

OUTLINE. n. A plan or sketch of the main points of a piece of writing. In an *outline*, the main ideas are arranged in an organized sequence.

PLAIN ENGLISH. Spoken English. To use *plain English*, write as if you were talking, rather than writing. Plain English is the opposite of jargon and is never stilted, pompous, or flowery.

PLOT. A series of events and actions, causes and effects, arranged to advance a story.

POINT OF VIEW. The angle, such as a physical location in time and space, from which something is seen, or an attitude toward a subject. *Point of view* also refers to writing in the first person ("I"), second person ("you"), or third person ("he sat . . ."). "Third person omniscient point of view" refers to the all-knowing narrator, who can say what's in the minds of the characters (e.g., Grace sat on the beach, wondering if David would come).

RÉSUMÉ. A summary of your experience, education, qualities, and qualifications. When you apply for a job, you present your *résumé* to the prospective employer.

RISING ACTION. Events in a struggle leading to a crisis and to the climax or turning point of a story.

SATIRE. Humorous writing exposing human follies. *Satire* can ridicule gently or savagely.

SCENE. A single situation or dialogue in a piece of writing. The *scene* is also the place where something happens.

SETTING. The locale or time period in which something takes place.

SHORT STORY. A unified short narrative, usually under 10,000 words. A *short story* generally tries to create a single strong impression.

SKETCH. (1) v. To jot down details, main points. (2) n. A brief outline or short descriptive essay.

STORY. A narrative account of what happened, either true or fictitious.

STRUCTURE. How something is arranged or put together. The *structure* is the framework of a story, article, essay, or poem, with all the parts in a certain order.

STYLE. A way of using language which expresses the spirit and personality of the writer. *Style* is your unique way of putting thoughts and impressions into words. Your style might be "breezy" or "upbeat" or "spellbinding."

SUMMARY. A short, comprehensive statement of the main points.

SUSPENSE. Uncertainty and tension about "what happens next?"

TECHNIQUE. The method used to achieve a certain effect, the "how" of writing well. A writer's *techniques* might include varying the length of sentences and paragraphs, or using comparisons, or dialogue.

THEME. The main idea or message. A short essay is sometimes called a *theme*.

THESIS. A theory or proposition to be proven, involving research and documentation. A *thesis* is also a dissertation or long essay exploring a subject extensively.

TONE. (1) Modulation of the voice (e.g., a "demanding" tone

of voice). (2) The manner of expression which reveals a writer's attitude toward her subject or reader. For example, a writer's tone might be sarcastic, or inspirational, or condescending.

TRANSITION. A way of getting from one point to another in what you're writing. A *transition* might be a word or passage connecting one part with the next.

UNITY. A totality of related parts held together by some organizing principle, method of presentation, or dominant impression. When your writing has *unity*, there is a sense of the parts fitting together to form a whole.

Appendix: Correct Format of Letters and Memos

Heading or Letterhead

Today's date

Inside Address
   Recipient's name, title if desired, company, address

Salutation
   Dear Mr. Jones:
   Dear Personnel Director: (That is, Dear Title and Last
      Name followed by a colon)

Body

Complimentary Close
   Sincerely yours followed by a comma

Typed Name of Sender

Sender's Job Title, if appropriate

Notations

> *FS/mw* writer's initials/typist's initials
>
> *Enc.* or *Encs.*, or the words *Enclosure* or *Enclosures*
>
> cc: Janet Johnson
>   Mark Smith
>
> Carbon copies or photocopies go to whom?
> Use *c.* when indicating one copy to one person.

A MODEL LETTER IN FULL-BLOCK STYLE

Household Warehouse Unlimited, Inc.
85 Windom Avenue
Manchester, CT 00000
(203) 123-3211

June 1, 19—

Mr. John Jenkle, President
Jenkle Electronics
134 MacLuhan St.
Hartford, CT 00000

Dear Mr. Jenkle:

We'd like to carry your heaters in our chain of stores.
Please send us the following information about Model
205:

- specifications
- cost
- safety record
- parts list

I've enclosed a description of our company. We need
this information by July 1, when we decide which new
products to stock. Thank you for responding quickly.

Sincerely yours,

Brad Ratchet,
Purchasing Agent

BR/hs
Enc.
cc: Matthew Cory
        Erica Kane

A MEMO IN FULL-BLOCK STYLE

Use a heading that tells **DATE, TO, FROM, SUBJECT.** In full-block style, all parts line up at the left margin. If you have a list, block it in the center. Writers can sign their initials next to their typed names, as below. There's no salutation or complimentary close in a memo. Notations are the same as for letters.

DATE: January 12, 19--

TO: All Sales Personnel

FROM: Tom Smith, Sales Manager *TS*

SUBJECT: A New Way to Process Orders

On February 1, we're changing the way we process orders. These changes will eliminate unnecessary paperwork, speed the processing of orders, and result in better service for our customers.

Attached are a list of steps to follow when placing an order. Keep it on your desk for reference.

Please sign this page and return it to me by January 20 so I know you received these changes. If you have any questions, call me at Ext. 505. Thank you.

Enclosure

Index

About the Author

DR. FRAN WEBER SHAW is the author of several books and numerous articles, and has won national awards for her writing. She is an Associate Professor of English at the University of Connecticut at Stamford. After graduating Phi Beta Kappa and *magna cum laude* from Barnard College, she was both a Danforth Fellow and a Woodrow Wilson Fellow at Stanford University. She earned a Master's degree from Stanford and a Ph.D. from the Union Institute. A writing consultant to Fortune 500 companies and a former Madison Avenue copywriter, Dr. Shaw is also the creator of *Write It Up!*, a self-teaching video course for business writers (call 1-800-621-2131). Fran Shaw lives in Connecticut with her husband and son and is at work on a new book of poetry and short essays.